CAMBRIDGE MUSIC HANDBOOKS

Brahms: *A German Requiem*

CAMBRIDGE MUSIC HANDBOOKS

GENERAL EDITOR Julian Rushton

Cambridge Music Handbooks provide accessible introductions to major musical works.

Brahms: *A German Requiem*

Michael Musgrave

Professor of Music
Goldsmiths College, University of London

Published by the Press Syndicate of the University of Cambridge
The Pitt Building, Trumpington Street, Cambridge CB2 1RP
40 West 20th Street, New York, NY 10011–4211, USA
10 Stamford Road, Melbourne 3166, Australia

First published 1996

Printed in Great Britain at the University Press, Cambridge

A catalogue record for this book is available from the British Library

Library of Congress cataloguing in publication data applied for

ISBN 0 521 40200 X hardback
ISBN 0 521 40995 0 paperback

SE

For Mary

Contents

Contents

Illustrations

Preface

The *German Requiem* made Brahms's international name. Previously known to a limited audience as an often problematic successor of Schumann in his extended piano and chamber works, he gained an entirely new audience, and earned comparison with Bach and Beethoven. Though long considered a major challenge to performers, the work quickly established itself in the repertory and has held a secure place ever since, despite changing fashions in choral music through the twentieth century. Nonetheless, it came to be associated with a certain stolidity and worthiness. Only of recent years has there been a fresh realization of its individuality of text and structure, as well as its sheer beauty of sound and line, first with the investigations of historical and stylistic scholarship, and latterly with the attention of performers using the forces and playing styles of the period. This book aims to reflect these trends as well as offering further detailed examination of the music itself. The individuality of the *Requiem* emerges from its history, in its links to the distant past and its unusual text; its structural mastery in the way this text and the musical ideas are balanced and integrated; its performance traditions through the reactions of critics and through a range of recordings made over the last fifty years up to the present.

Acknowledgements

I am indebted to several individuals and institutions in carrying out my research: to Kurt Hofmann, director of the Brahms Institut, Lübeck, for access to valuable scores, manuscripts and printed documents, and for his unique knowledge of Brahms's connection with North Germany; to the Stadt- und Universitätsbibliothek, Hamburg, and the Staats- und Universitätsbibliothek, Bremen, for access to scores and contemporary reports, especially to Dr Ann Kersting of the Bremen Staats- und Universitätsbibliothek for providing information from the archives of the Bremer Singverein; to the British Library, Royal College of Music Library and New York Public Library for access to specialized literature; to the Gesellschaft der Musikfreunde, Wien, for permission to reproduce from the autograph full score (Plate 2) and from the photograph of Brahms (cover); to the Wiener Stadt- und Landesbibliothek for permission to reproduce the text-sheet of the *Requiem* and to Dr Otto Biba and Frau Ruth Racek (its former owner) for identifying its present location (Plate 1); to the Society of Authors on behalf of the Bernard Shaw Estate for permission to reproduce from the writings of George Bernard Shaw; to Stephen Keeley for preparing the music examples; to Julian Rushton for more helpful comments and suggestions than I ever adequately acknowledge, and Lucy Carolan for her painstaking editing of the text; finally to Herr Gustav Abel and the Brahms Gesellschaft, Baden Baden for the invitation to work in the Brahmshaus Studio, Lichtenthal, Baden Baden. I count it a particular privilege to have been enabled to bring this book towards completion in the house in which Brahms finished many of his greatest compositions, and not least, in the summer of 1866, the *German Requiem* itself.

Abbreviations

In Chapters 2 and 3, the following abbreviations are used in discussing tonality, harmony and formal divisions.

Major and minor keys and chords are indicated by upper- and lower-case numerals and characters as follows (for example in the key of F, as on p. 56):

I	IV	vi	VII	I	III	I
F	B♭	d	D	F	A	F
F major	B♭ major	D minor	D major	F major	A major	F major

Raised and lowered diatonic relationships are indicated by ♯ and ♭ respectively (for example in movement 6):

c:	V	♯iii	♯vi	IV	I	V
	G	e	a	F	C	G

Neapolitan relations (key/chord on flattened degree of II and VI)	Np
First (large idea)	A
Second (large) idea	B
First (smaller) idea	a
Second (smaller) idea	b
Multiple ideas	a1, a2
Variations of ideas	a1 var, a2 var
Transition	Tr
Modulating passage	Mod
Unclear or temporary keys, ideas or subjects	shown by a bracket, e.g. (III)

Introduction

I will admit that I could happily omit the 'German' and simply say 'Human'[1]

Concept

Brahms's frank admission to Carl Martin Reinthaler, the organist of Bremen Cathedral, before rehearsals for the first performance of his *German Requiem* (prepared by Reinthaler, conducted by Brahms) captures the essence of the work, as well as pointing to its originality.[2] For not only did Brahms substitute the German language for the more familiar Latin of the Requiem Mass, but he also substituted for the traditional sources an entirely independent compilation of texts with no liturgical purpose. By 'human' Brahms indicates to Reinthaler[3] that the primary emphasis of his text is on the comforting of the living and not the spiritual destiny of the departed. Nonetheless, the fact that his text had such strongly Christian associations naturally prompted enquiry as to its theological meaning, and the nature of his own beliefs. Thus the orthodox Reinthaler sought to persuade Brahms to give his work a more specifically Christian content when contemplating with him the preparation of performance, writing on 5 October 1867:

You stand not only on religious but on purely Christian ground. Already the second number indicates the prediction of the return of the Lord, and in the last number but one there is express reference to the mystery of the resurrection of the dead, 'we shall not all sleep'. For the Christian mind, however, there is lacking the point on which everything turns, namely, the redeeming death of Jesus. Perhaps the passage 'death, where is thy sting' would be the best place to introduce this idea, either briefly in the music itself before the fugue, or in a new movement. Moreover, you say in the last movement, 'blessed are the dead which die in the Lord from henceforth', that is, after Christ has finished the work of redemption.[4]

Reinthaler's suggestion fell on deaf ears. Brahms replied that he had knowingly passed over such passages as St John, Chapter 3, verse 16 ('for God so loved the world that he gave his only begotten son'), while he had selected others 'because I am a musician, because I needed them, and because I cannot dispute or delete a "from henceforth" from my revered poets'.[5] Brahms was surely not being evasive in this answer. He would doubtless have found it difficult to defend his choices in theological terms. The choice of familiar words was more an expression of cultural identity than a theological statement. He read the Bible as a repository of experience and wisdom in memorable literary form, rather than as defining the Christian creed. Indeed, there is no reference to Christ anywhere in the text of the Requiem, though Christ's words are quoted from St Matthew's gospel at the very outset and from St John's gospel in the fifth movement. But the textual content must have continued to cause some concern to the Bremen cathedral authorities and it is notable that the programme of the first performance included amongst its additional items movements from some of Handel's *Messiah*, including the aria 'I know that my Redeemer liveth'.[6]

Brahms retained this independence of outlook throughout his life. Though baptized and confirmed in the Lutheran faith,[7] 'nothing made [him] more angry than to be taken for a conventional believer on the basis of his religious compositions'[8] and he liked in later years to point out the 'heathen' character of some of his preferred texts.[9] The conviction of outlook which emerges from his choice of texts was based on an intimate knowledge of the Christian scriptures, inclining as much to the Old Testament as to the New and also drawing on the Apocrypha.[10] It was this knowledge which imparts to the text of the *Requiem* its great power and focus, since Brahms draws together many related and complementary fragments from diverse sources.[11] Deeply held thoughts and sentiments which emerge repeatedly in his work are prominent: the bleak reality of the transience of life, the need of comfort, the hope of some ultimate happy resolution, the reward for effort. The *Requiem* offers the most comprehensive selection of such texts in a single Brahms work. In so doing it also stands at an important point in his spiritual development, at least as defined through the texts he set. Those before the *Requiem* tend to be more orthodox than the later ones, complete texts from the Old or New Testaments or hymn-texts of the Lutheran tradition. But from the 1870s, beginning with the major works for chorus and orchestra to secular texts, and continuing with the motets Op. 74 and Op. 110 to religious texts, a more recurrent pessimism creeps in. Two works serve to place the sentiments of the *Requiem* in a broader perspective: the *Begräbnisgesang* (*Burial Song*) Op. 13, for chorus and wind band, written in 1859, about ten years before completion of the *Requiem*, and the *Vier ernste Gesänge* (*Four Serious Songs*) for baritone and piano, written thirty years later in 1896 at the end of his life. The *Burial Song* is a single-movement setting of the graveside hymn of the Lutheran Burial Service 'Nun laßt uns den Leib begraben . . .' ('Now let us bury the body . . .') beginning (like the second movement of the *Requiem*) with the contemplation of the common fate of man and beast. It speaks of the confidence of the faithful in the resurrection of the departed one and ends with the hope of eternal rest in the comfort of the Saviour. By the time Brahms had selected the texts of the *Four Serious Songs* the context of the imagery had changed. After three texts which intensify the picture of man's fate and which eventually welcome death for those with nothing to hope for, there is a resolution into St Paul's great hymn to Christian love in his first letter to the Church at Corinth: 'now abideth faith, hope and love, but the greatest of these is love'.[12] Thus, human love concerned Brahms at the end of his life more than a contemplation of the unknowable.

Brahms's choice of texts places his *Requiem* in a unique position within the tradition of nineteenth-century choral works with orchestra. His major German predecessors Beethoven, Schubert and Schumann all expressed their religious sentiments in music through the Latin texts of the Mass or Requiem Mass. Even Schumann, who was the most dedicated to the use of German, and who also noted the idea of a 'German Requiem' as a future project (though Brahms claimed to know nothing of it),[13] wrote all his German 'oratorios' to secular texts, including his *Requiem for Mignon*, taken from Goethe's *Wilhelm Meister*. The tradition from which Brahms made his text goes much further back: to the Protestant church music of the Baroque, most notably of J. S. Bach and Heinrich Schütz. Both anticipate Brahms's choices of texts, texts that were then very familiar to church musicians. Schütz set 'Die mit Thränen säen' twice (in the *Psalms of David*, 1619, and in the *Geistliche Chormusik* of 1648), 'Wie lieblich sind deine Wohnungen' once (in the *Psalms of David* of 1619 (for double choir a 4)) and 'Selig sind die Toten' in the *Geistliche Chormusik* of 1648. Several Bach cantatas draw on these and on other of the *Requiem* texts in the German originals or in paraphrase form. Furthermore, these texts also appear in non-liturgical compilations in works for specific devotional or funeral uses. Schütz's *Musicalische Exequien* is in three sections, of which the third combines the text of the German Nunc Dimittis, 'Herr, nun lässest du deinen Diener' with that of 'Selig sind die Toten'. Schütz's work is a German-language Requiem of 1636, a *Teutsche Begräbnissmissa*. Of Bach's works which compile individual texts, Cantata 106, 'Gottes Zeit ist die allerbeste Zeit' (known as 'Actus Tragicus'), has been seen as an obvious precursor,[14] a small 'German Requiem' in six movements, of which the third uses the text of Brahms's third movement in an alternative version from Psalm 90, verse 12, 'Herr, lehre uns bedenken, daß wir sterben müssen, daß wir klug werden' (Lord, teach us to know that we must die, so that we may become wise'). The tradition continued into the nineteenth century: as well as Schumann's concept, Franz Schubert composed a *Deutsches Requiem* for his brother's professional use.[15] This continuity obviously adds another dimension to Brahms's use of the indefinite article in his title, *Ein deutsches Requiem*: one particular choice of texts within a tradition of vernacular settings.

Against this German background it becomes of interest that Brahms used the Latin term 'Requiem' at all, rather than a designation more characteristic of his Baroque predecessors, such as 'Geistliche Chormusik' or 'Trauerkantate'. It may have been prompted by the work's symphonic scope, by the desire to place it alongside the great requiem mass settings of the past; indeed, it has some structural parallels with the Latin mass which are not part of the Protestant inheritance (though its emphasis is certainly very different, and it notably offers up no prayers for the dead). Musical settings of the Requiem text differ widely in their allocation of text to individual musical movements, as well as in some textual content, though some, like the Brahms, fall into seven movements.[16] But, like Brahms's, most have a recall of the opening movement at the end (to 'Requiem aeternam dona eis Domine' in the first and last, with the related text 'dona eis requiem sempiternam' in the Agnus Dei) and have somewhere near the centre the contemplation of blessedness (the 'Sanctus' in the Mass, movement 4 in the Brahms), as well as reference to the 'tuba mirum' text (in the 'Dies Irae' of the Latin and movement 6 of the Brahms). In placing the work in the fuller perspective of familiar religious texts it is also of note that Brahms's final text 'Selig sind die Toten' is in the final section of the Lutheran funeral service, and other parallels exist with this service, as well as with its counterpart in the Anglican liturgy. The major feature which separates the Brahms text from that of the Latin Mass is the recurrence of its basic themes. The Mass's very lengthy sections with their diverse imagery have often stimulated dramatic musical settings. But Brahms's text is compact and focused, with several key ideas constantly in play.

History

What little is known of the *Requiem*'s origin is based on Brahms's correspondence and on reminiscences published after his death. The correspondence shows ongoing work during April 1865 and from February to August 1866, with revision from August to December 1866. The first reference to the work comes in a letter from Brahms to Clara Schumann of 'April 1865' in which he encloses a choral movement from 'a kind of German Requiem'. Brahms's letter of Monday 24 April 1865 refers again to the work, also mentioning a second movement, as well as a first which was already conceived orchestrally, and quoting their texts:

Just have a look at the beautiful words with which it begins. It is a chorus in F major without violins but accompanied by a harp and other beautiful things . . . I compiled the text from passages from the Bible. The chorus I sent you is number four. The second is in C minor and is in march time . . . I hope that a German text of this sort will please you as much as the usual Latin one. I am hoping greatly to produce a sort of whole out of the thing and wish for enough courage and energy to carry it through.[17]

Of the fourth movement he comments (with typical self-deprecation) 'it is probably the weakest part of the said German Requiem, but . . . it may have vanished into thin air before you come to Baden'.[18] In her reply of 1 May she responded 'the chorus from the Requiem pleases me very much, it must sound beautiful. I like it particularly up to the figured passage, but not so much where this goes on and on' (bb. 134–6 of the fourth movement).[19] Only in Brahms's reference to the march of the second movement as being 'in C minor' rather than the published B♭ minor do these comments conflict with the movements 1, 2 and 4 that we know (and this could be explained as a printer's error in the published edition of the correspondence with Clara).[20] That the music of the present third movement was also part of the scheme, though not mentioned by Brahms, seems implicit in the identity of movements 1, 2 and 4; presumably it was not mentioned because it was still sketchy or incomplete. Though Brahms vouchsafed knowledge of the work to Clara, he begged her at this stage 'not to show the enclosed fourth movement to Joachim',[21] which suggests that he had still not advanced enough with the work to wish to encourage expectations of it. Nothing more is heard of the *Requiem* until February of the following year, when the composition of the remaining movements of a six-movement work and completion of the existing ones emerges in regular sequence whilst Brahms was staying in Karlsruhe, Winterthur, Zurich and finally in Baden Baden. The main part of the third movement was completed between February and 18 April, the fugue between 18 April and the beginning of June. Movements 5 and 6 (which became movements 6 and 7 in the final version) were then completed between the beginning of June and 17 August, when Brahms wrote at the end of the score 'Baden Baden summer 1866'.[22] From then until 24 October he worked further on editing the full score at Baden, and allowed Clara to hear more of it, also inviting Albert Dietrich to do so.[23] Between 25 October and December he prepared a vocal score which he gave to Clara on 30 December.[24]

Although a press report prior to the first performance in Bremen in April

1868 indicates that it was then known that the second movement dated from much earlier,[25] it was only when the reminiscences of Albert Dietrich were published in 1899, two years after Brahms's death, that more specific information became available. Dietrich states that the movement was originally part of the Sonata/Symphony in D minor of 1854: 'the slow scherzo after became transformed into the funeral march in the *German Requiem*'.[26] The two-piano Sonata had been begun in February 1854 and had been planned in three or possibly four movements. Sometime towards the summer of that year Brahms began to orchestrate it as a symphony. This work was then abandoned and its first movement reworked to form the first movement of the Piano Concerto in D minor, to which two new movements were added to complete the work later published as Op. 15 in 1859.[27]

Dietrich's description of the 1854 movement as a 'slow scherzo' has always aroused curiosity, since it seems a contradiction in terms. However, it can be explained by the movement's symphonic origin, the term relating to form not to style. In a parallel example from only four years previously, the second movement of a symphony, Schumann's *Rhenish* (1850), also associates the title Scherzo with a movement much slower than normal, here a slow Ländler in 3/4. Brahms's key (B♭ minor relative to a tonality of D minor) would also have fitted a post-Beethoven symphonic scheme. Less clear in meaning is Dietrich's further characterization of the theme, communicated to Kalbeck and widely quoted since, as being 'in Sarabande tempo'; this is puzzling, since the typical rhythm usually results in a change of harmony on the second beat and not the third, as in the *Requiem* movement.[28] The press comment, presumably informed by Dietrich or even Brahms himself, merely relates that the movement was similar 'in outer form' to the later *Requiem* movement. Whether the march contained the distinctive theme given to the chorus to the words 'Denn alles Fleisch' cannot be decided from Dietrich's brief remarks. The familiar view of Brahms's first biographer Max Kalbeck that the choral part was added as a 'counterpoint' to the instrumental march has no support in fact;[29] on the other hand, Brahms stated that both this choral material and the opening bars of the first movement are based on a Lutheran chorale melody: a clue to the work's hidden background? The implications of this comment are pursued in Chapter 2 (pp. 26–34). No hard evidence of what took place in the intervening eleven years at present exists, though much Brahms literature still reflects the conjectural view of Kalbeck that the work had assumed the form of a 'Trauerkantate' comprising movements 1–4 of the present work in some form of completion by 1861.[30] Kalbeck's specificity of date is based on an interpretation of a single sheet which contains the entire (seven-movement) text of the

Requiem on the verso of a draft for the fourth of the *Magelonelieder* (at the end of the first volume), known to have been composed in 1861 in Hamburg; this he sees as having been written in two stages, Nos. 1–4 in 1861 and Nos. 5–7 later. The relevance of this sheet almost certainly belongs to a much later stage when Brahms was considering the position of the newly composed fifth movement (see p. 10 and note 42). That so original a work may have assumed some preliminary form, however, seems feasible, and the likely influences upon its growth cannot be ignored in considering its nature (these issues are also pursued in Chapter 2, pp. 31–4).

Since the *Requiem* was not written to commission or for any public event, no performance was envisaged immediately after its completion. Indeed, Brahms was still reluctant to advertise it at all, being more concerned with the reactions of his trusted circle to its unusual conception. Only Clara, Joachim and Dietrich seem to have been intimate to its emergence, though a slightly broader circle, possibly including Clara's friends in Baden and Brahms's former teacher Eduard Marxsen in Hamburg, came to know of it when it was first completed. It was to Dietrich that he vouchsafed the full score itself when contemplating the first performance, in a letter written shortly after 7 June 1867.[31] It was natural that he should have first have thought of a North German city such as Bremen and a Protestant cathedral for the first performance of such a work. And there were also professional reasons: he still had strong contacts in the north and retained aspirations towards the position of director of music in a major city, which such a performance would advance. Moreover, Reinthaler had a fine reputation as a choir trainer and Brahms could expect careful preparation of his work. He writes to Dietrich on 30 July 1867:

I start tomorrow on a walking journey with my father through upper Austria, I do not know when I shall be back. Keep the enclosed Requiem until I write to you, Do not let it out of your hands and write to me very seriously by and by what you think of it. An *offer* from Bremen would be very acceptable to me. [But] it would have to be combined with a concert engagement. In short, Reinthaler must probably be sufficiently pleased with the thing to do something for it. For the rest I am inclined to let such matters quietly alone. I do not intend to worry myself about them.[32]

Brahms's concern about the manuscript was understandable. As Florence May observes in her biography of the composer, 'there is a trace of nervous anxiety in this letter which leaves little doubt that Brahms had within him the consciousness that in the *German Requiem* he had transcended all his previous achievements and that he was even unusually anxious to secure a favourable opportunity for hearing a new work. Up to now it had only been submitted to Frau Schumann's drawing room and a few enthusiastic friends of the Baden circle.'[33] By the time Brahms returned to Vienna and requested the return of his manuscript from Dietrich, his friend had sent it to Bremen.[34] His hope for a Bremen performance – Brahms's correspondence with Reinthaler begins in early October from Vienna – was not to have been in vain.[35] But important as the possibility of Bremen clearly was to Brahms, he also had his contacts in Vienna, where he had lived frequently since 1862. Through his contact with the conductor of the Gesellschaft der Musikfreunde, Johann Herbeck, a performance of movements 1–3 was arranged for 1 December 1867, in a programme dedicated to the memory of Schubert which also included a performance of movements from the *Rosamunde* music. The orchestral and choral parts were prepared from the beginning of October, and the soloist in the third movement was Rudolf Panzer of the Imperial Chapel.[36]

The long-standing plans with Bremen had reached finalization by the beginning of 1868, and Brahms informed his publisher Rieter-Biedermann that the first performance would take place in the Cathedral on Good Friday, 10 April, with Julius Stockhausen as baritone soloist, he himself conducting.[37] Brahms was still apparently willing to receive advice on the work from close confidants; for example, he wrote to Marxsen to request some comments that might help to improve the work, including something on the pedal fugue of the third movement.[38] Brahms took great interest in the rehearsals, which began in early February. He offered to come and play the difficult piano reduction in the vocal score. His own involvement helped to stimulate interest and the two leading papers carried advance notice of the first performance and accounts of the work and of its composer's importance, for about ten days before. The advertisement for the day before the first performance, Thursday 9 April, listed the additional items in the programme of the 'Geistliches Konzert' (Sacred Concert) to be conducted personally by the composer, the proceeds of which were to go to the benefit of the widows' and orphans' fund of the city. The additional items were to be performed during a break between movements 4 and 5 (that is, 4 and 6 of the present numbering) and after the work. In this break Joachim played three items: the slow movement of Bach's Violin Concerto in A minor with orchestra, an Andante by Tartini and his own arrangement of Schumann's song 'Abendlied', both with organ accompaniment. After the end of the *Requiem*, Joachim was joined by his wife, the alto Amalie Weiss, in the aria with obbligato violin 'Erbarme dich' from Bach's *St Matthew Passion*. In addition Weiss sang the aria 'I know that my redeemer liveth' from *Messiah* and the choruses 'Behold the Lamb of God' and 'Hallelujah' were performed. The performance was a great success and the cathedral was full, with upwards of 2,500 people in attendance, including many of Brahms's friends and other distinguished musicians from all over Germany and abroad. The deep significance of the event for Brahms and his circle emerges clearly from Clara's diary. She travelled to Bremen on 9 April, partially in the company of the Joachims, and arrived in Bremen whilst Brahms was taking the rehearsal. 'Johannes was already standing at the conductor's desk. The Requiem quite overpowered me . . . Johannes showed himself an excellent conductor. The work had been wonderfully prepared by Reinthaler. In the evening we all met together – a regular congress of artists.' Of the performance itself she says 'the Requiem has taken hold of me as no sacred music ever did before . . . As I saw Johannes standing there, baton in hand, I could not help thinking of my dear Robert's prophecy, "Let him but once grasp his magic wand and work with orchestra and chorus", which is fulfilled today. The baton was really a magic wand and its spell was upon all present. It was a joy such as I have not felt for a long time.'[39] The second performance was given on Tuesday 28 April at the Bremen Union, Reinthaler now conducting, and with the baritone solo sung by Franz Krolop; the programme included Beethoven's Seventh Symphony and a Weber aria.

The fifth movement

During the month following the Bremen premiere, Brahms completed another movement for soprano solo with chorus and orchestra, which became No. 5 in the final published sequence (the former Nos. 5 and 6 becoming 6 and 7 respectively). He wrote the manuscript in Hamburg, where he had gone to stay with his father and to add the final touches to the Bremen score for publication. It was seemingly completed by 24 May 1868, when Brahms sent the corrected full score to Rieter-Biedermann, writing 'Now a seventh number has to be added, No. 5, soprano solo, with about 16 bars of chorus. I shall send this number later as I have to have it written out first and have to look for a place where I can have it played over to me, for money and kind words. Therefore I note that it occupies seventeen pages in my full score and six pages in the vocal score; you can therefore plan accordingly.'[40]

The reason for the late addition of the movement to an already performed work has always prompted speculation, not least because of the text, with its reference to the comfort of a mother, which has been widely connected with the death of Brahms's own mother, little over three years before on 2 February 1865: indeed, according to Florence May, Brahms told Hermann Deiters that 'when writing [the movement] he had thought of his mother'.[41] However, the evidence that the text and music of the movement were selected and conceived after (rather than the music composed after) is by no means certain. The documentary evidence provided by the text-sheet (see pp. 6–7 and Plate 1) permits several interpretations. The most literal is that the text was conceived as part of the whole before the first performance, since the sheet contains the entire text with tempo markings for movements 1 and 2 which predate not only the published score but the many revisions in the autograph full score and part-autograph vocal score which were used for the rehearsals and first performance:[42] it might thus be connected with the period when Brahms is known to have borrowed a large biblical concordance, seemingly to check his text and its sources, during final work on the *Requiem* at Zurich in summer 1866.[43] However, the distinction between the texts of movements 1–2 and 3–7 can also be interpreted to suggest that 3–7 were added later to provide the complete text (perhaps for easy reference), either before the first performance or after. Whether Brahms's equivocation over the order of movements 4 and 5 (first reversed, then restored) was part of this process is also an open question. But if both added text and changed numbering were written down after the first performance (thus before Brahms notified his publisher of the new movement numbered '5' on 24 May 1868), one wonders why he needed to complete the entire text of a work, the score of which (with the draft/final copy of movement 5) already contained it. Doubt also attaches to the assumed chronology of the composition of the added movement. The period from roughly mid April to 24 May at the latest seems very short for the conception and execution of such an individual movement which complements the sentiment and musical structure of the whole so profoundly.[44] Knowledge of Brahms's protracted working processes and the fact of the very personal nature of the conception suggest prior planning of text and music, if not yet of final execution, a fact perhaps confirmed in the confidence with which he stated to his publisher, when notifying him of the added movement, that 'with luck it makes the work even more of a whole'.[45]

In the light of this background, the more interesting aspect of the fifth movement might become, not why did Brahms 'add' it, but why did he hold it back? Several explanations would suggest themselves. First, he needed the experience of the work in performance to decide on the appropriateness of a predominantly solo movement: the work at this stage was still (as it would seem to have been for a long preceding period) a work in progress. Second, he knew he required a movement to this text, but was not sure of its musical form. Here the evidence of Marxsen's involvement may well fit in. May cites that 'a well known musician of Hamburg, to whom Marxsen, after studying the score of the German Requiem for a second time, entrusted the responsibility of

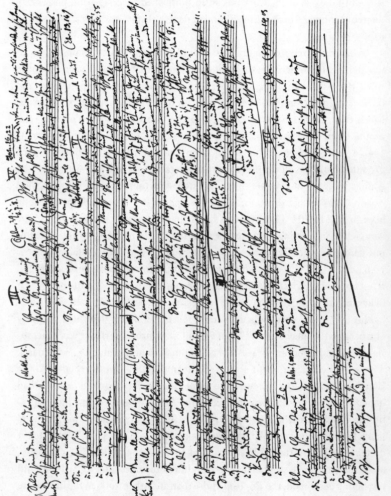

Plate 1 Complete text of the *German Requiem* in Brahms's hand (Wiener Stadt- und Landesbibliothek)

carrying it back from his house in Altona to Brahms in the Anscharplatz, told the present author positively, when she visited Hamburg in 1902, that the soprano solo was added by Marxsen's suggestion'.[46] But perhaps the most convincing view is that the content was too personal for him to give it public exposure until the rest of the work was an accomplished success, that it possesses a degree of intimacy both musically and in its text that he was at first reluctant to expose publicly.

An earlier dating for the text does not of course diminish its possible relationship to his mother's death, but it does suggest that she influenced the entire work. But even in this larger context, a direct connection between the event and the concept and composition seems difficult to sustain: in chronological terms, barely two months covers the time between her death and Brahms's first revelation to Clara of the title and description of much of the music of movements 1–4. A much longer period would seem characteristic of Brahms for such extended music (as all the preceding consideration of the work, apart from the connection with his mother, has suggested). Furthermore, he had had good reason to expect her death for some time before it occurred, as she had long been in frail health. Thus it seems likely that the event was a stimulus to the completion of existing ideas, rather than the source of them, with the text of movement 5 especially associated with her in his mind. This certainly accords with Deiters's recollection that Brahms was 'thinking of her' in this passage and is not contradicted by Clara Schumann's comment that 'we all think he wrote it in her memory though he has never expressly said so'.[47]

However, if the event was important, it seems unlikely that there was only one personal influence on the *Requiem*, and more probable that it was a memorial to other important figures from Brahms's youth, including Schumann. This (despite her comment above) seems implicit in Clara's reaction to the Bremen rehearsal. Brahms was to comment in 1873 to Joachim (who he had hoped would arrange a performance of the *Requiem* for a Schumann celebration in Bonn, but who failed to do so, to Brahms's irritation) 'you ought to know how much a work like the *Requiem* belongs to Schumann. Thus I felt it quite natural in my inmost heart that it should be sung for him.'[48] Schumann, more than anyone else, transformed Brahms's fortunes after an arduous and restricting childhood; the *Requiem*, more than any other work, made him aware of his need to come to terms with his growing achievement. Thus the work may perhaps be seen ultimately as a requiem for his own youth, an account of his spiritual and musical journey thus far. There surely has to be a reason why he chose to make such a personal composition his first great work, rather than the first symphony which had been so long in progress.

On completion of the additional movement, Brahms was immediately anxious for a run-through and approached several friends for a soprano soloist, but without success. The first performance of the fifth movement was on 17 September 1868 in Zurich at a private performance in the Tonhalle-gesellschaft with Ida Suter-Weber as soprano and Friedrich Hegar conducting. The scores and parts appeared in the following months. The autograph score (from which the full score was made) has a remarkable mixture of page sizes, because, as he told May and several others, 'at the time I wrote it I never had enough money to buy a stock [of paper]'.[49] Though Brahms subsequently expressed the wish to revise the work, he never did so, chiefly (in the recollection of Mandyczewski) because it had become so familiar.[50]

2

The work as a whole

The biblical text: sources and structure

The text of the *German Requiem* is taken from the original text of Luther's Bible, with modernized spelling and punctuation and some emendations.[1] The following English translation is of this text,[2] rather than an English biblical source (the English Authorized Version and New English Bible differ from the Luther Bible significantly in details of syntax and emphasis). The sources given in the following key are in the order of their appearance in the work; they are also used in the discussion of the music in Chapter 3. Numbers in brackets refer to musical subdivisions within sources.

Key to sources

A	New Testament	The Gospel of St Matthew, Chapter 5, verse 4
B	Old Testament	Psalm 126, verses 5–6
C	New Testament	The First Letter of Peter, Chapter 1, verse. 24
D	New Testament	The Letter of James, Chapter 5, verse 7
E	New Testament	The First Letter of Peter, Chapter 1, verse 25
F	Old Testament	Isaiah, Chapter 35, verse 10
G	Old Testament	Psalm 39, verses 4–8
H	Apocrypha	The Wisdom of Solomon, Chapter 3, verse 1
I	Old Testament	Psalm 84, verses 1, 2, 4
J	New Testament	The Gospel of St John, Chapter 16, verse 22
K	Apocrypha	Ecclesiasticus [The Wisdom of Jesus, son of Sirach], Chapter 51, verse 27
L	Old Testament	Isaiah, Chapter 66, verse 13
M	New Testament	A Letter of Hebrews, Chapter 13, verse 14
N	New Testament	The First Letter of Paul to the Corinthians, Chapter 15, verses 51–2, 54–5
O	New Testament	The Revelation of John, Chapter 4, verse 11
P	New Testament	The Revelation of John, Chapter 14, verse 13

Ein deutsches Requiem	A German Requiem
nach Worten der heiligen Schrift	to words of the Holy Scriptures
für Soli, Chor und Orchester	for soloists, choir and orchestra
(Orgel ad lib.)	(organ ad lib.)

Soloists: Baritone (in movements 3 and 6) and soprano (in movement 5); Chorus: SATB; Orchestra: 2 flutes, piccolo, 2 oboes, 2 clarinets, 2 bassoons, contrabassoon (ad lib.), 4 horns, 2 trumpets, 3 trombones, tuba, timpani, harp (at least two players), strings, organ (ad lib.)

I

['Ziemlich langsam und mit Ausdruck'; **C**; F major to texts A and B: a choral and orchestral movement with orchestral introduction, mainly homophonic with some imitative writing. An A B A form of text and music with sectional variation]

Selig sind, die da Leid tragen,	A	Blessed are they that have sorrow,
denn sie sollen getröstet werden.		they shall be comforted.
Die mit Thränen säen,	B(1)	They that sow in tears,
werden mit Freuden ernten.		shall reap in joy.
Sie gehen hin und weinen	B(2)	They go forth and weep
und tragen edlen Samen,		and carry precious seed
und kommen mit Freuden		and come with joy
und bringen ihre Garben.		and bring their sheaves with them.
[Selig sind . . .]	[A]	[Blessed are they . . .]

II

['Langsam, marschmäßig', Bb minor; 3/4: a choral and orchestral march with introduction and interludes to text C; 'Etwas bewegter', Gb, 3/4: a 'trio' for chorus and orchestra, more lightly scored, to text D, followed by da capo of the march; 'Un poco sostenuto', Bb major, 4/4: a transitional passage to text E, leading directly into 'Allegro non troppo', Bb major, 4/4: a choral and orchestral movement with prominent use of fugal devices to text F]

Denn alles Fleisch es ist wie Gras	C	For all flesh is as grass
und alle Herrlichkeit des Menschen		and the splendour of man
wie des Grases Blumen.		is like the flower of the field.
Das Gras ist verdorret		The grass withers
und die Blume abgefallen.		and the flower falls.
So seid nun geduldig, lieben Brüder,	D	So be patient, dear brothers,
bis auf die Zukunft des Herrn.		until the coming of the Lord.
Siehe, ein Ackermann wartet		See how the farmer waits

15

auf die köstliche Frucht der Erde		for the precious fruit of the earth
und ist geduldig darüber,		and is patient for it
bis er empfahe		until he receives
den Morgenregen		the Spring rains
und Abendregen.		and the Autumn rains.
[Denn alles Fleisch . . .		[For all flesh . . .
die Blume abgefallen.: D.C.]		and the flower falls. D.C.]

Aber des Herrn Wort	E	Yet, the word of the Lord
bleibet in Ewigkeit.		stands for evermore.
Die Erlöseten des Herrn	F	The redeemed of the Lord
werden wieder kommen		shall return
und gen Zion kommen mit Jauchzen;		and come to Zion with rejoicing;
ewige Freude wird über ihrem Haupte sein,		eternal joy shall be upon their heads,
Freude und Wonne werden sie ergreifen,		they shall obtain joy and gladness
und Schmerz und Seufzen wird weg müssen.		and pain and suffering shall flee away.

III

['Andante moderato', D minor, ₵: a movement for baritone solo, chorus and orchestra to text G, continuing in D major/minor, 3/2 with transition to pedal fugue in D major, ₵ for chorus and orchestra to text H]

Herr, lehre doch mich,	G(1)	Lord, let me know
daß ein Ende mit mir haben muß,		that I must have an end,
und mein Leben ein Ziel hat,		that my life has a term,
und ich davon muß.		and that I must pass on.
Siehe, mein Tage sind	G(2)	See, my days
einer Hand breit vor dir,		are as a hand's breadth before you
und mein Leben ist wie nichts vor dir.		and my life is as nothing before you.
[Herr, lehre doch mich . . .]		[Lord, let me know . . .]
Ach, wie gar nichts sind alle Menschen,	G(3)	Truly, all men that still walk the earth
die doch so sicher leben.		are hardly as anything.
Sie gehen daher wie ein Schemen,		They go hence like a shadow
und machen ihnen viele vergebliche Unruhe;		and all their noise comes to nothing,
sie sammeln, und wissen nicht		they heap up their wealth
wer es kriegen wird.		but do not know who will inherit it.
Nun, Herr, wess soll ich mich trösten?		Now, Lord, how shall I find comfort?
Ich hoffe auf dich.	G(4)	I hope in you.
Der Gerechten Seelen sind in Gottes Hand,	H	The righteous souls are in the hand of God,
und keine Qual rühret sie an.		and no torment touches them.

IV

['Mäßig bewegt'; E♭ major; 3/4: a choral and orchestral movement to text I; mainly homophonic with a fugal development]

Wie lieblich sind deine Wohnungen,	I(1)	How lovely are your dwellings,
Herr Zebaoth!		Lord of Sabaoth!
Meine Seele verlanget und sehnet sich	I(2)	My soul longs and faints
nach den Vorhöfen des Herrn;		for the courts of the Lord.
mein Leib und Seele freuen sich	I(3)	My body and soul rejoice
in dem lebendigen Gott.		in the living God.
Wohl denen, die in deinem Hause wohnen,		Blest are they that dwell in your house,
[Wie lieblich . . .]		[How lovely . . .]
die loben dich immerdar.	I(4)	they praise you evermore.
[Wie lieblich . . .]		[How lovely . . .]

V

['Langsam'; G major'; ₵,: a movement in A B A form for soprano solo, chorus and orchestra, the A section to texts J and L (chorus), the modulating central section to texts K and L (chorus)]

Ihr habt nun Traurigkeit;	J	You now have sorrow,
aber ich will euch wieder sehen		but I will see you again,
und euer Herz soll sich freuen,		and your heart shall rejoice,
und eure Freude soll niemand von		and your joy shall no man take
euch nehmen.		from you.
Sehet mich an:	K	Look on me:
Ich habe eine kleine Zeit		For a short time I have had
Mühe und Arbeit gehabt		sorrow and labour
und habe großen Trost funden.		and have found great comfort.
Ich will euch trösten,	L	Thee will I comfort
wie einen seine Mutter tröstet.		as one whom a mother comforts.
[Ihr habt nun Traurigkeit . . .]		[You now have sorrow . . .]

VI

['Andante'; C minor; ₵: a choral and orchestral passage in marchlike idiom to text M, continuing with solo/arioso to text N (1–2); 'Vivace'; C minor; 3/4: a fast choral homophonic passage to text N (3–4); 'Allegro'; C major; ₵; a choral and orchestral fugue to text O]

Denn wir haben hie keine bleibende Statt,	M	For we have no abiding city
sondern die zukünftige suchen wir.		but we seek one to come.
Siehe, ich sage euch ein Geheimnis:	N(1)	Behold, I tell you a mystery:
Wir werden nicht alle entschlafen,		We shall not all sleep,
wir werden aber alle werwandelt werden;		but we shall all be changed;
und dasselbige plötzlich, in einem Augenblick,		and that quickly in a moment
zu der Zeit der letzten Posaune.	N(2)	at the sound of the last trumpet.
Denn es wird die Posaune schallen,	N(3)	For the trumpet shall sound,
und die Toten werden auferstehen unverweslich,		and the dead shall be raised incorruptible,
und wir werden verwandelt werden.		and we shall be changed
Dann wird erfüllet werden	N(4)	Then shall be fulfilled
das Wort, das geschrieben steht:		the word that is written
Der Tod ist verschlungen in den Sieg.		Death is swallowed up in victory
Tod, wo ist dein Stachel?		Death, where is your sting?
Hölle, wo ist dein Sieg?		Hell, where is your victory?
Herr, du bist würdig	O(1)	Lord, you are worthy
zu nehmen Preis und Ehre und Kraft,		to receive praise and glory and power,
denn du hast alle Dinge geschaffen,	O(2)	for you have created all things,
und durch deinen Willen haben sie das Wesen		and by your will were they created
und sind geschaffen.		and have their being.

VII

['Feierlich'; F major; **C**. a choral and orchestral movement to text P in A B A form, followed by recapitulation of the reprise of the first movement as a coda after the main movement to text P(1)]

Selig sind die Toten, die in dem Herrn sterben,	P(1)	Blessed are the dead which die in the Lord
von nun an,		from now on
Ja der Geist spricht, daß sie ruhen von ihrer Arbeit;	P(1/2)	Yes, says the spirit, that they rest from their labours
denn ihre Werke folgen ihnen nach.		and their works follow after them.[3]

The text of the *German Requiem* is a significant creative achievement in its own right. Brahms's profound knowledge of the Scriptures is revealed in its close-knit fabric of individual passages drawn from sixteen chapters of ten books of the Old and New Testaments and the Apocrypha. Only the texts of movements 4 and 7 are taken entirely from one source, the Book of Psalms and the Revelation of St John respectively. The others draw on two or three books each. The spread of the sources shows that Brahms did not seek to take his subject from any one part of the Bible or topic within it, as was the case with such Protestant works of his era as Mendelssohn's *Elijah* or *St Paul* or Heinrich von Herzogenberg's *Die Geburt Christi*. Rather he relates his sources to themes of his own and creates a uniquely personal, non-dogmatic sequence of thoughts.

The opening thought is one of the most familiar of Christian texts, the second of the 'Beatitudes' in St Matthew's gospel, almost at the beginning of the New Testament. This thought finds its fulfilment in 'Blessed are the dead' (movement 7) from Revelation, at the end of the New Testament; connecting the two ideas is the vision of the resurrection and transformation of souls in 1 Corinthians (movement 6). If the essence of Brahms's spiritual journey lies in the New Testament, its elaboration draws heavily on the Old Testament. In this process, the Psalms are central. They appear in three of the first four movements (1, 3 and 4) and develop the opening idea, often in long passages – Psalm 84 provides the whole text for movement 4. The choice of the Psalms would have been as natural to Brahms as the expectation of hearing them in a religious work to his listeners: their poetry, expressing a wide range of human emotions – from self-doubt and insecurity to pure confidence and celebration – makes them the best-known book of the Old Testament. Brahms also favoured the Psalms in his shorter choral works to German texts; for example, the seven Motets Opp. 29, 74 and 110, and the *Festival and Commemoration Sentences*. The text from Isaiah (F) which concludes the second movement is one of sustained affirmation of confidence in God, and a similar sentiment in the Apocrypha serves a parallel purpose at the end of the third movement. In addition, the New Testament passages themselves incorporate parts of the Old. Texts C and E of the second movement appear in the First Letter of Peter, but as a quotation from Isaiah (Chapter 40, verses 6 and 7). Brahms's growing pessimism in later years led him to draw on such texts as the Book of Job and the Lamentations of Jeremiah in the Motet Op. 74/1, as well as on texts from Ecclesiastes and Ecclesiasticus in the *Four Serious Songs* Op. 121.

The deep unity resulting from the recurrence and variation of the textual themes of the *Requiem* is given vital focus by the use of symmetry. By placing the texts of deepest reassurance and consolation at the centre of the work, Brahms creates a kind of mirror structure in which the third division reinterprets the first. A pattern emerges with relations between movements 1 and 7, 3 and 6, 4 and 5 (so long as movement 2 can be seen as an elaboration and continuation of movement 1); this structure both reflects on the text's recurring themes and progresses towards a transformed conclusion. Movements 1–3 show the gradual elaboration of Christ's words 'Blessed are they that have sorrow, for they shall be comforted.' Text B of the movement glosses this, also introducing another equally powerful idea, that of reward for effort, in the line 'They go forth and weep . . . and come with joy and bring their sheaves with them.' The texts of the second movement extend and intensify these two ideas. The image of the sower of the seed is now related to man's common fate with the rest of the natural world in text C. Text D calls for patience, whilst retaining the nature imagery – 'see, how the farmer waits for the precious fruit of the earth and is patient for it till he receives the Spring and Autumn rains', the movement ending with a return to the passage used for C1 (its fourth line E). In the third movement the perspective shifts from that of the individual contemplating human transience through bereavement to that of the individual contemplating his own destiny, in the psalmist's injunction 'Lord let me know that I must have an end' which, after building to the question 'Now, Lord, how shall I find comfort', calls forth the response 'I hope in you' (text G(4), followed by an assurance of security for the righteous (text H). As in the previous movement, the concluding text is preceded by an affirmation which provides a transition between the texts of mourning and consolation.

Where the texts of the first three movements have juxtaposed despair and hope with increasing intensity, the middle two movements celebrate hope, likewise first through communal expression then individually. Movement 4 is entirely a song of praise for the state of blessedness to text I. Texts J and K of the fifth movement present, for the first time in the work, a voice of authority speaking comfort directly to the individual mourner; the identity of the voice is most strongly associated with a mother in text L. The sixth movement returns to the questioning of No. 3, though here harnessed more urgently to the prospect of a destiny to come in text M. As in movement 5, a voice of authority speaks to the individual or mourner, here of a changed state of being and of the destiny of human souls, in text N (1–3): 'Behold I tell you a mystery . . . we shall all be changed', resolving into a hymn of praise for the power of God to text O. Text P of movement 7 closely parallels that of movement 1, 'Blessed are they that have sorrow' becoming 'Blessed are the dead which die in the Lord', whilst also drawing on the reference to patience rewarded in No. 2, text D, in a more direct and profound way; the text 'Yes, says the spirit, that they rest from their labours and their works follow after them' thus emerges as the ultimate personal message of the work: that man must rejoice in his achievements. Here the state of blessedness for the mourner in movement 1 has been enhanced, both by the assurance of a spiritual transformation in movement 6 ('Blessed are the dead which die in the Lord from now on') and by the promise of a deserved rest after labour ('for they rest from their labours and their works follow after them').

Though all the texts of the *Requiem* are biblical and exist in a specifically Christian context there, Brahms can be seen considerably to weaken the Christian meanings through his precise selections and juxtapositions: his text sequences are interesting for what they omit as well as what they include. He focuses on comfort, hope, reassurance, and reward for personal effort, conspicuously avoiding judgement, vengeance, religious symbols and – above all – the sacrifice of Christ for human sin. In fact, he could have chosen the language of German classical or Romantic poetry to express many of these general sentiments, as he did later in the *Schicksalslied, Nänie* and *Gesang der Parzen*. His choice of biblical sources suggests the desire to draw particular truths from the Christian tradition, to make his own theology in the tradition of Lutheran preaching and biblical exegesis and to offer it through music in the spirit of the Lutheran cantata.

His independence is already clear at the outset. The Beatitudes, given in the Sermon on the Mount, show Christ indicating to his humble followers the great rewards of faith: gaining the kingdom of heaven, having the earth for their possession, seeing God, being sons of God. Brahms seems to claim the least of these rewards; simply the assurance that the sorrowful shall find consolation. In the second movement, the quoted Old Testament text is presented as a hymn to human transience, 'For all flesh is as grass . . .', whereas its context is that of a former state (represented by the use of quotation) which has been changed by divine intervention; 'You have been born anew, not of mortal parentage, but immortal, through the word of God' (NEB). The assurance of the return of God's people which ends the movement occurs without the mention of the divine vengeance (Isaiah 35, 4) through which the Way of Holiness is prepared. In movement 3, the psalmist's questioning of the purpose of his life appears as a response to the acknowledgement of his own sin. In the coda to movement 3, the affirmation that 'the righteous souls are in the hand of God' is presented without the original implication that this is through the agency of Christ and religious discipline: the preceding biblical passage is that 'after a little chastisement they will receive great blessings'.

Other passages play down images of divine power and symbols of religious belief. Thus the climax of movement 6, 'Lord, you are worthy to receive praise and glory and power', occurs in the Bible accompanied by the vivid imagery of the Book of Revelation, showing 'one who sits on the throne . . . the twenty elders of the temple falling down before the throne, the one on the right with a scroll'. Even the elision of one verse from Psalm 84 (whose nature imagery would seem to have offered Brahms even more scope for musical elaboration than he chose to use) may well have been for its images of religious practice: in 'Wie lieblich sind deine Wohnungen' . . . the omitted verse 3 reads 'even the sparrow finds a nest when she rears her brood beside thy altar, O Lord of Hosts . . .'

Movements 5 and 6 offer the most striking examples of meanings changed through selection. In movement 6 Brahms has heavily edited 1 Corinthians 15, verses 51–7, by deleting references to physical resurrection (as he does also in the second movement) as follows: 'the perishable must be clothed in the imperishable, and what is mortal must be clothed with immortality' followed by the Christian association of resurrection and the concept of salvation from sin: 'the sting of death is sin, and sin gains its power from the law; but, God be praised, he gives us the victory through our Lord Jesus Christ' (NEB). Thus Brahms conceives resurrection as a changed state, not through sacrifice, and with no reference to that of Christ. Reinthaler's comment, 'but the work lacks the whole point on which the Christian religion turns, the sacrificial death of Christ', shows how forcibly these omissions struck him. In movement 5, only one of the three short texts refers directly to the love of a mother for her child. However, Brahms has imbued the whole movement with this sense: while the soprano sings texts J and K, the words 'Thee will I comfort . . .' are delivered simultaneously by the choir, commenting on the solo voice. In fact, the first text, J, 'You now have sorrow . . .' comes from a passage in which the imagery of motherhood is very strong – the metaphor of the pain of labour and the joy of birth are used here to depict the anxiety at the death of Christ but the joy of his resurrected appearance – whereas in its proper context the third text, L, uses the love of a mother only as a metaphor for the love of the holy city, Jerusalem: 'as a mother comforts her son so will I comfort you and you shall find comfort in Jerusalem' ['then you may suck and be fed from the breasts that give comfort', verse 11 preceding]. The second text, K, 'look on me . . .', contains no mother imagery; it occurs in a passage praising the joy of study and thus reinforces the idea of patience rewarded. But this theme too could be connected to Brahms's mother, for she has been credited with passing on to her son a sensitivity towards literature. The result is a personal hymn to consolation and comfort which removes the words from a Christian context, the voice of a God figure or of Christ, and gives them by implication to the voice of a mother, realized in the music by a soprano solo. It is difficult, in the light of the work's background, not to see this hymn as a very intimate tribute to Brahms's mother and her influence upon him.

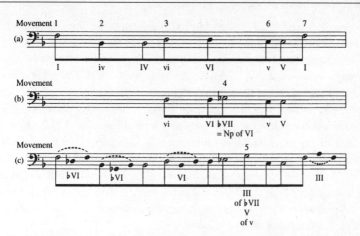

Ex. 1 Large-scale tonal structure in three stages (stemmed black noteheads show change of mode)

The music: large-scale form and historical background

In commenting to Reinthaler that 'I chose my texts because I am a musician',[4] Brahms clearly implies that for all the care with which they had been put together, his texts could not ultimately stand alone. Certainly in the case of movement 7, brevity seems to imply elaboration by musical means in order to balance the other movements; indeed, it cannot be known at what stage any of the texts were already associated in his mind with musical material. In a purely musical sense, the work satisfies as a self-sufficient structure. Brahms constructs large-scale movements with overall A B A or A B shapes, but his handling of them is far from stereotyped: the interaction of text and music produces formal subdivisions which are capable of several interpretations (these are discussed further in Chapter 3).

The large-scale formal contour is most obviously defined through tonal means. The tonal structure of the seven movements may be seen in three stages of elaboration (a, b, c). In the first stage, if F major is seen as the key of the work as a whole, then movements 1, 2, 3, 6 and 7 represent the progression I–IV–vi–V–I (see list of abbreviations, p. x). Modal contrast within these movements then creates the enhanced basic scheme of I–iv/IV–vi/VI–v/V–I. These modal contrasts are commonplace in Brahms's music. The progression I–iv–[II–V] appears as early as bb. 33–6 in the opening movement and frequently thereafter. The transformation of the submediant (relative minor) to major, vi/VI, simply applies the 'tierce de Picardie' relationship to a whole section. The least usual relationship is that created by the initial placing of a minor tonality on the fifth degree (C minor) before the dominant V (C major) in movement 6, a transformation of the dominant function made possible through their own shared dominant. A second level of elaboration (b) is provided by the addition of the tonality of E♭ major (♭VII) in movement 4. This has both an expressive and structural role. From the expressive standpoint, the sudden semitone shift from the seemingly total affirmation of D in the last section of the third movement reveals a new and unexpected tonal realm. Structurally it can be seen as slightly less unusual if placed in the context of the original six-movement scheme; here it emerges as a Neapolitan decoration of D, linking directly to the C minor which opens the sixth movement, its own relative minor, en route for the work's large-scale dominant, C major–F major: vi/VI–Np(♭VII)–v/V–I.

A final stage (c) is provided by the 'additional' fifth movement in G major which greatly enhances the link between E♭ and C minor by complementing the ambivalent dominant harmonic function of the opening of the latter movement, where the composer purposely avoids confirming the tonality until the second main section 'Vivace'. The tonal ambivalence through modal juxtaposition in the first section greatly enhances its effect as a transitional passage, thus reflecting its text and strengthening its eventual resolution to C minor. It also has the effect of introducing into the work's large-scale structure the tonal relationship which dominates the internal relations of the movements, and thus adding to organic coherence: mediant and submediant relations appear in all movements except No. 6 and the pivotal E♭ movement, again reflective of Brahms's methods in other works of the period (drawing largely on late Beethoven and Schubert): I, F–D♭; 2, B♭ minor–G; 3, D minor–B♭ minor; 5, G–B♭; 6, C minor–E minor; 7, F–A. In addition to these major structural contrasts, mediant inflections are to be found in many other passages of lesser structural prominence.

The work's tonal coherence is matched by an equally clear process of thematic planning. It manifests itself most clearly in a conspicuous shape noted by several writers, and appropriately described by Grasberger as the 'Selig' ('Blessed') motive:[5] that which appears in the upper part in the first choral entry of the work to the words 'Selig sind', bb. 15–17, and is then repeated and extended for the whole of the line 'Selig sind, die da Leid tragen', the figure then freely inverted to initiate the second paragraph, bb. 29–30 (Example 2a, i–iii). The more precise inversion of the motive appears in diminished note values to initiate the new figure which marks the opening of the coda at bar 144, which is then combined with the ascending original. This passage is des-

Ex. 2 The 'Selig' motive and examples of its thematic use

tined to be further reworked as the closing paragraph of the last movement (movement 7, bb. 152–4) and the main theme of the movement clearly derives from it, also employing the original motive in bb. 2–4 (Example 2b). The original and inverted shapes of the motive are so conspicuous within the main themes of the work that the use of the 'Selig' motive must be regarded as an intended means of unity. It usually appears at the openings, but is also present within the themes themselves (Example 2c). In the fourth movement, the use of the inversion of the first three bars of the choral melody in the orchestral introduction offers particular evidence of this consciousness of planning (Example 2c). In the several cases where the motive appears as part of the counterpoint to a new idea, the process suggests a second compositional stage; the motive generating the new theme. The fact that this feature appears more strongly in the later movements may perhaps suggest their generation at a later stage in the chronology of thematic derivation. That the coda of the first movement combines the original and inverted/diminished motives might also suggest that this crucial passage in the work's structure came relatively late in the compositional process, the result only of a reflection on the potential of previously worked material (Example 2d).

Though Brahms never appears to have mentioned this unifying feature, the fact that he made a really striking claim for the role of another thematic element that is far less obvious to the listener inevitably attracts attention, since it has much wider relevance for the work's origins. In discussing the use of a chorale melody in the *Triumphlied* with the choral conductor Siegfried Ochs, Brahms referred to the *Requiem*: Ochs recalls 'to my comment . . . he answered in his rather sarcastic manner "if you can't hear it, it doesn't matter much. In the first bars and in the second movement you can find it. It is a well-known chorale"'. Ochs remarks that after this indication, the origin of the chorale was easy to deduce, comparing the opening bars in F major with the chorale melody in F minor 'Wer nur den lieben Gott läßt walten'[6] (incomplete in his version, complete in Example 3), and pointing out that the relation is even closer in the second movement, 'Denn alles Fleisch es ist wie Gras'. Ochs mentioned the chorale on two later occasions. In the first he ascribes its identification directly to Brahms and claims Brahms's indication of a larger role for it ('He mentioned to me that the chorale "Wer nur den lieben Gott läßt walten" lay at the root of the entire work'), whilst in the second he simply refers to the funeral march in the second movement by this name.[7]

Given that we know the second movement to contain the oldest extended music, and that this must have related closely to the essential contour of the existing choral part in order to have preserved its identity in recollection, its

Ex. 3 Role of the chorale melody 'Wer nur den lieben Gott läßt walten' as noted by Ochs

choral melody must bear closest relation to the chorale. This conclusion is not necessarily challenged by its lack of an initial dominant upbeat, since one source of the chorale records an initial tonic,[8] and Brahms may have known both versions; it also shares the chorale's distinctive final perfect cadence to the dominant, 2–5 descending, which is lacking in simpler derivatives. If the first movement is seen as composed after the second, which all evidence suggests to have been the case, then its opening theme can be seen as a transformation to major of a minor original, a less clearly related derivative: just a single line of 1–2–3–2–1 in the major with an undecided ending 7–6–7. It seems important that the only other chorale-like melody in the work, the 'Vivace' section of the sixth movement, also relates directly to the shape of the second movement (though without the strong cadence): it is in a stark outline of 1–2–3–2–1 (with internal repetition) in the minor, which at its repetition takes the dominant upbeat 5–1–2–3–2–1. In the preceding passage (bb. 34–62) the solo line, taken up in the orchestra, can also be seen as an elaboration of this, linked by the same textual continuity. If all these minor versions are conflated, one basic outline can be drawn from them: that is, 5–1–2–3–2–1–5 in the minor, essentially identical with the chorale. The relationship does not extend beyond the first phrase of the chorale. The requirements of Brahms's texts create a new, extended consequent in the second movement, and extension through repetition in the 'Vivace' of the sixth. Other examples seem to reveal the chorale outline without the upbeat. In the third movement, the second section and reprise of the opening (from b. 33 to b. 104) are dominated by a shape given first in the major by the soloist and eventually in the minor, the shape also used as a recurrent accompaniment figure (which has obvious relation to the triplet decoration of the chorale in the 'Vivace' of movement 6). Its distinctive minor third, D–F, can be seen as retained in a more distant variant of the chorale

27

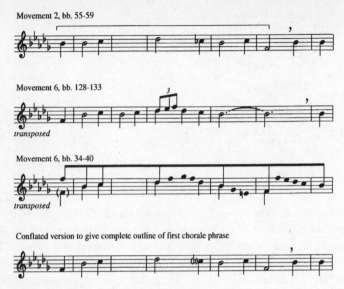

Ex. 4 Role of the chorale melody 'Wer nur den lieben Gott läßt walten' in movements 2 and 6

phrase at the opening of movement 6 (bb. 3–7), the minor second, E♭, recalling the lowered second degree of the chorale in the second movement. The soprano solo of the fifth movement can also be seen to shadow the choral phrase (in the major, especially if the alternative version of the second bar is taken), and the shape is also used in the bass to the orchestral introduction. However, even if we acknowledge that Brahms's remark only referred to the first phrase of the chorale, his claim that it lay 'at the root of the work' is not literally justified. Beyond the cited passage, it is the 'Selig' motive and its derivatives which secure the work's thematic unity. Yet since there is an intimate association between the two ideas in the work's opening bars, the claim can be seen to be true in a deeper structural sense. Thus, a three-stage process of derivation might be drawn from the evidence: (1) first phrase of the chorale in skeletal form in the minor; (2) transformation of (1) to major with varied outline and no clear cadence; (3) derivation of the 'Selig' motive, either as a counterpoint to the chorale or from the skeleton of the harmonic setting of the chorale, bb. 1–3. (See Chapter 3 for details of this relationship.)

The lack of consonance between Ochs's first and second statements regarding the chorale has caused some doubt as to its identity (since Brahms never actually specified its title on the occasion when he made the remark and there is

Ex. 5 Role of the chorale outline without upbeat in movements 3, 6 and 5

Ex. 6 Chorale melody 'Freu' dich sehr, O meine Seele'

no evidence of more than one occasion), and one writer has openly challenged
Ochs's deduction. Christopher Reynolds suggests that he drew a mistaken
conclusion, which he then relayed as fact, and thus that the issue of the
chorale's identity remains open. In seeking to deduce the identity, he points
rather to the first movement as the source and notes its very close association
with the chorale 'Freu' dich sehr, O meine Seele' as part of a broader argument
concerning the relationship of the funeral march to the Sonata/Symphony of
1854.[9]

Judged in purely thematic terms, the question must remain open. Neither of
the musical passages quoted by Brahms fits the same chorale source perfectly –
nor, indeed, could this have been his intention, since they are presented as
totally different themes. Even if Ochs did invent the chorale's identity (which
seems to give him too little credence – he was a collaborator with Brahms in the
performance of his works), the only clue to the meaning of Brahms's comment
and the creative influence behind it must lie in clarifying why Brahms chose a

chorale theme at all, and why he felt the need to acknowledge that it existed. Had Brahms made no comment on the origin of the great choral theme of the funeral march of the second movement, one would certainly think no more of it, but probably ascribe it to that class of chorale and folk-like melodies which permeate his work and which were so basic to his style; the stark chorale-like presentation, 'choralmäßig' as it is often described, would simply suggest a public and religious version. But he was surely doing more than merely pointing out the resource of his thematic process to Ochs. If the chorale is taken as a melody which symbolizes certain types of text through its association with them in settings by other composers, than a range of possible background stimuli to these movements emerges: the tradition of chorale composition. For it seems inconceivable that a composer with Brahms's reverence for traditional forms had no preliminary models or general conceptions in mind for a work of such striking individuality. There is every evidence that it grew by stages. His reference to movements 1–4 being in existence when he first informed Clara of the work in 1865 and his hope to 'make something out of it if I have enough energy' clearly suggests this, as does the fact that the funeral march was transformed from an earlier version. The presence of a chorale melody in two movements of the Requiem immediately establishes a link to Brahms's other chorale compositions of the period. The motet Op. 29/1 (1860) is a chorale fantasia on 'Es ist das Heil uns kommen her'; the motet Op. 74/2 is a set of strict variations after Bach on the chorale text and melody 'O Heiland, reiß die Himmel auf' (first mentioned 1870, but written earlier). Additionally, a chorale melody ('Herr Jesu Christ, du höchstes Gut') has been suggested as providing the thematic material of the *Geistliches Lied*, Op. 30, of 1856,[10] and some of Brahms's folksong arrangements of the period were of chorale melodies and texts.

Given this devotion to chorales and chorale-based composition, the proposition that Brahms wished to provide a much more individual realization of such a work – one which rather than highlighting a given melody and associated text, used it in a more subtle way within a more individual formal structure consistent with his own musical language and personality – is not far-fetched. Indeed, he did just this in the *Begräbnisgesang*, the main idea of which is a cumulative funeral march which uses a strikingly chorale-like melodic outline, though this is shared between the orchestra and choir and presented at the outset, rather than introduced later, as in the funeral march of the *Requiem*. Brahms's remark on the theme to Grimm – 'I don't have to tell you that I have not used any chorale or folk melody'[11] – could be taken as ironical, since its predominant outline (minor key) 1–2–3–2–1 – ♯7–1–2–3–2 is close to that of the first phrase of the chorale 'Erhält uns, Herr, bei deinem Wort'[12] (though Brahms shifts the accentuation fundamentally to give it a different effect), or literal, as indicating that the chorale-like melody was his own. The funeral march of the *Requiem* can clearly be seen as an expansion of this compositional principle to a different theme with a much more personal chorale text, and the whole work as an expansion of the chorale-cantata tradition into a large-scale modern context.

The association of Brahms's supposed chorale melody with its texts seems to provide the vital clue to its development. For this melody and its associated texts in Bach cantatas would have been well known to Brahms in the period of the suggested formation of his idea. Cantata 21, 'Ich hatte viel Bekümmernis' ('My spirit was in heaviness'), which he performed in 1858 at Detmold, has both the melody of 'Wer nur den lieben Gott läßt walten' (lit. 'Who only lets beloved God rule') and the text 'be rested my soul, how profitless our bitter sorrow – all our pain and woe' in an inner movement in 12/8, thus paralleling the chorale text (verses 2 and 3) 'what can these anxious cares avail thee . . . only be still and wait his leisure'.[13] Brahms would have known this work from the new *Bach Gesellschaft* edition which appeared from 1851 and to which he was a subscriber. But more striking is Cantata 27, which sets the same melody to the words 'Who knows how near my end shall be' ('Wer weiß wie nahe mir mein Ende'): a paraphrase of the biblical text which Brahms used in the third movement of the *Requiem*, 'Lord let me know that I must have an end' ('Herr, lehre doch mich . . .'). Moreover, both Bach and Brahms take the unusual step of changing the rhythm of the chorale from common time to 3/4, and their orchestral settings resemble each other.[14]

The suggestion is, then, that Brahms's transformation of his 1854 funeral march into a choral march was prompted by his discovery of Bach's cantatas. And it could not be refuted even if no chorale or chorale-like melody was present in the 1854 march:[15] this is ultimately impossible to assert, since Brahms almost certainly reworked his material to give it greater individuality and coherence. One notes, for example, the subtle and organic use of the opening plagal progression iv–i at the harmonization of the choral entry later in the phrase, accommodating the distinctive Cb of the melody (Eb minor – Bb minor/Ab minor – Eb minor). Equally, a remnant of the 5–1 melodic opening of the chorale (if this is how Brahms knew it best) might be discerned in the opening bass notes, F–Bb. If the chorale was added later with its parallel text, it might explain why Brahms adds the balancing word 'es' to his biblical source 'Denn alles Fleisch ist wie Gras' (he retains the original form in his title). The melody and its textual associations certainly had powerful connections for

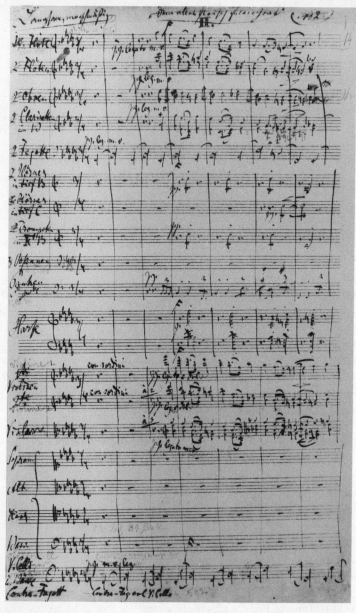

Plate 2 The opening of the second movement of the *German Requiem* in Brahms's full autograph score

Ex. 7 Role of the chorale melody 'Wer nur den lieben Gott läßt walten' in Bach, Cantata 27 and *Requiem*, movement 2

Brahms in more modern and personal contexts than that of the Bach cantatas. Mendelssohn used the harmonized chorale with orchestra for the comtemplation of the stoning of Stephen in *St Paul*. Nor was the association with suffering and hope for guidance limited to religious music. Schumann had used the melody with a poetic text of similar sentiment in the Heine *Liederkreis* Op. 24, No. 8, 'Anfangs wollt' ich fast verzagen . . .' ('At first I thought I should never be able to bear it. Now I have, but never ask me how'), with a new continuation to the borrowed first phrase, just as Brahms does in these cases. The Schumann tragedy, which seems closely associated with the Sonata of which the funeral march was part, would have given this chorale a very appropriate role in the work. Furthermore, the outline of the complete melody to 'Denn alles

Brahms: Op 121/1 'Denn es gehet...'

Brahms: German Requiem, Movement 2

transposed

Ex. 8 Thematic parallel between (a) Brahms, 'Denn es gehet dem Menschen wie dem Vieh', Op. 121/1 and (b) *Requiem*, movement 2

Fleisch . . .' reappears much later in the first of the *Four Serious Songs*, which uses a parallel text, 'Denn es gehet dem Menschen wie dem Vieh' ('for it goes the same with man as with the beasts').[16] Thus the association of melody and text, the association with Bachian and later usage, and the personal dimension in Brahms's life present a fabric of relationships which seems indeed to show the melody as the key to the work's gradual evolution.

3

The individual movements

Overview

The forms of the individual movements of the *German Requiem* take on special interest in the light of the fact that Brahms selected his own texts. Rather than merely 'setting' the words, Brahms chose them to ensure a certain pattern of formal unity and diversity; they conditioned musical realization more precisely than the often longer and more diverse texts of the liturgical Requiem Mass[1] and gave Brahms opportunity for the variation of familiar forms and subtle long-term integration which typify all his work. In this the *Requiem* resembles his many solo songs,[2] where the structure and accentuation of the poem are generally apparent in a rounded musical form (though in the *Requiem* the metrical freedom and length of the biblical texts presuppose a much larger formal space and more expansive musical processes). As also in his solo songs, Brahms has little place for word-painting for itself. Rather, he prefers to embody the illustrative and (more often) symbolic aspect of the texts through structural musical devices, which can be more elaborately employed in the larger choral and orchestral domain: the texts are notable for their concentration on a group of related images and avoidance of the pictorial emphasis which would encourage musical digression. Within these confines, however, the composer still varies the emphasis on music and text, so that in some passages the words are more obviously accommodated to the musical form than in others.

The integration of words and music finds a parallel in the integration of musical idioms. The language of the *Requiem* is often 'secular', as it integrates instrumental and vocal as well choral forms: for example, orchestral march and dance, lyric song and recitative. And though Brahms does follow tradition in concluding some movements with impressive fugues or fugally influenced sections, the technique is not associated with any obvious 'liturgical' style (as in the work of his German predecessors), but is related to a wide variety of contrasted elements. The orchestra plays a central role in this integration: it is rarely mere accompaniment, but typically shares material with the soloist and chorus, though it also creates some passages of sharp individuation. The *Requiem* represents a crucial step in Brahms's orchestral development (indeed it sometimes suggests the more adventurous directions in which he still might have moved at this stage of his career). The orchestra is the largest he had used by this time: in addition to his normal double woodwind (with optional contrabassoon), four horns, three trombones and tuba, he specifies 'at least two harps' as well as organ 'ad lib.'[3] and explores the uses of the instrumental groups and divisi and muted effects, especially in the strings, more than in any other work. In the following discussion of the movements, the large three-part division already observed (movements 1–3, 4–5, 6–7) is retained. Separate assessment is given to issues of textual and musical structure and to features of musical style and expression, which, taken together, cover the formal and expressive progress of the work.

Movements 1–3: textual and musical structure

The choice of an appropriate form for movement 1 is crucial to the realization of the design of the *Requiem* as a whole. It has to introduce and integrate the short text-phrases which embrace the work's message, yet also serve a longer-term structural purpose when its opening music is recalled in movement 7 – at the same time without the complete recapitulation that would obviously lessen the structural effect of this recall. Brahms's solution is to design a movement which exists in two simultaneous musical forms (Form 1 and Form 2 below): on the one hand, as a broad ternary form (A B A) resulting from its clear textual/musical recapitulation; on the other, as an alternating variation form which successively reinforces the three distinct thoughts of texts A, B(1) and B(2).

Movement 1

Text		A	B(1)	(2)	(2 cont.)	A	A
Form 1	A		B			A	
Form 2	a1	a2	b	a1 var	b var	a2	a
Key: F	I	I	♭VI	I	♭VI	I	I
Bars	I	15	47	65	78	106	144

Form 2 is given added subtlety by the use of a composite first musical idea (a1 and a2) in bb. 1–14 and bb. 15–17 and 19–28. At first hearing, the orchestral introduction a1 gives the impression of being quite distinct from the unaccompanied choral passage a2 which responds to it with the opening of text A, 'Selig

Ex. 9 Movement 1: variants of ideas a1 and a2

sind'. Yet these ideas are deeply unified since the choral passage realizes the
harmonic skeleton of the opening, a relationship which becomes clear as the
orchestra further responds to the chorus in bb. 17–19, the passage thus
revealed as a recomposition of bb. 1–5 (Example 9). The greater animation of
text B(1) 'Die mit Thränen säen . . .' is matched by a more active musical idea b
in D♭ major, introduced suddenly by an interrupted cadence at b. 47 (the tonic
only being restored at the end of this section, b. 65). The reason for Brahms's

Ex. 10 Movement 1: variants of idea b

matching of text A to music a2 at b. 15 becomes clear at the entry of text B(2) at
b. 65 (see Examples 9 and 10): this is set not to a new musical idea, but successively to ideas a1 and b, which thus become rhythmically varied by the addition
of new text. Thus the composer has integrated all three texts by the use of
common or closely related musical material based on only two main ideas, a1
and b. He produces, in the process, a particularly subtle parallel between texts
B(1) and B(2) which, though beginning differently (the second a variant of the
first), come to identical musical climaxes at the respective words 'werden mit
Freuden ernten' and 'und kommen mit Freuden und bringen ihre Garben' (bb.
47–63 and 78–96).

The return of the opening text and music at b. 106 to make the recapitulation of the large (A B A) form is the crucial structural event of the movement,
since it is from this section that the first movement will be reintroduced as a
coda to the entire work in movement 7. In order to increase the effect of the
reprise of music a2 to text A (and perhaps to prepare the listener for this eventual goal) ideas a1 and a2 are recalled to the opening words 'Selig sind' in a
passage of tonal retransition, beginning in D♭ at b. 96 (which becomes ♭VI of
the tonic, F, at b. 106). But when this moment of recall is reached, the material
is memorably reinterpreted: the choral idea a2 is now given to woodwind an
octave higher than in the original vocal setting, with only the choral altos
initially participating, and providing the lowest part of the harmony. Text A

Ex. 11 Movement 1: recapitulation and coda

continues to serve through the shortened recapitulation, the final phrase
'getröstet werden' being used extensively for the coda (bb. 144–58).

The relation of text to musical structure in the second movement is completely different. Instead of a form designed to integrate short text-phrases, a
boldly sectional musical treatment makes a feature of the much greater length
and continuity of the text: first a self-contained triple-time 'march' with an
introduction (which serves as a ritornello) for text C; then an equally independent 'trio' for the contrasting text D (followed by a da capo of the march);
finally a transition, to text E, which leads to a lengthy concluding section
including fugal writing to text F. The change from tonic minor to major for the
transition and concluding section serves to create a complementary section in a
large A B form (see Form 1 and Form 2 below).

Movement 2, bb. 206-208 'Die Erlöseten des Herrn'

Movement 2, bb. 75-82 'so seid nun geduldig...'

transposed

Ex. 12 Movement 2: relation of 'trio' (transposed) to 'fugal subject'

Movement 2

Text	C	D	(C)	E	F1	F(2)	F(3)
Form 1	A			tr	B		
Form 2	a	b	a	tr	c1	c2	c3
Key: b♭:B♭	i	♭VI	i	I	I		
Bar	1	75	126	198	206	219	233

The sectional structure of the text lends itself easily to the wholesale musical repetition Brahms employs in order to build the massive climax invited by its imagery. Thus the whole opening text C 'Denn alles Fleisch' is repeated to an intensified statement of the march a1 (now *ff*, SATB in stead of *pp*, ATB) and the whole double statement of a1 is repeated after the 'trio' 'So seid nun geduldig . . .' In contrast, this 'trio' is set with only brief textual repetition as a small ternary form with a coda, in the submediant major, G♭, providing total contrast with the intensity of the march. The real resolution of the pessimism of text C comes only at the transition to the concluding section at the end of the da capo of a1 'Aber des Herrn Wort . . .' Indeed, in the process Brahms appears to draw a textual association through music between text D and text F ('Die Erlöseten des Herrn . . .') by emphasizing a triadic rising pattern to the octave in both themes – an 'open' shape in obvious contrast to the preceding material. The three thoughts of text F provide the contrasted elements of the partly fugal concluding section: F1 ('Die Erlöseten des Herrn') the 'exposition' (bb. 206–18); F2 ('Ewige Freude . . .') and F3 ('Freude und Wonne . . .') the transition to the dominant and quasi 'second subject' towards and in the dominant (bb. 219–32). The 'exposition' returns as a greatly elaborated recapitulation from b. 269 (first appearing in F major as a temporary foil to the true tonic B♭, in paired stretto) and the 'Freude' passage is transposed to conclude in the tonic rather than the dominant (d/F = g/B♭). The setting of text F(3) is not recalled in the recapitulation, thus giving its syncopations and expressive chromaticism (bb. 233–68) the function of a dramatic central section. Rather, emphasis is now given to the word 'ewige' (partially omitted previously to achieve the choral syncopations at bb. 219–22), in a tranquil pedal coda, in which the entire phrase 'ewige Freude' is passed from one voice to another whilst the orchestra does likewise with the opening fugal phrase ('Die Erlöseten des Herrn').

In the third movement the tonal contrast between the main body of the movement and the concluding fugue and its preparatory transition likewise creates a large A B form. However, because the fugue is much shorter (35 bars from a total of 207) and formally constrained by its pedal (without contrast or modulation), its function is more in the nature of a coda than a balancing major section. More formal variety lies in the A section in response to its lengthy text; here text and music proceed more continuously than in the previous movements, without any large-scale recapitulation of the opening material (though there is a small-scale reprise of the opening text G(1) which effects a clear subdivision of text/music of the first part of section A (a1, a2, a1)):

Movement 3

Text	G(1)	G(2)	G(1)	G(3)[1]	[2]	G(4)	H
Form 1	A					tr	B
Form 2	a1 (solo/chorus)	a2 (s/c)	a1 var (s/c/orch)	b1	b2	c(tr)	d(1 2 3)
Key: d:D	i	VI mod i		I	i mod	I	I
Bars	1	33	67	105	118	164	173 183 196

The formal character of the A section arises from the introduction of the solo baritone voice, which appears in response to the personal voice of text (G) 'Herr, lehre doch mich . . .' The close interaction of solo and chorus now facilitates a more flexible disposition of text, in which immediate repetitions of phrases give the music greater momentum and direction. But equally, reprise of G(1) is used to reinforce the basic thought which opens the movement: the powerful orchestral cadence which dies away to nothing (bb. 93–104) makes an emphatic break before texts G(1) and G(2) 'Siehe, meine Tage' and the next main division of text G(3) 'Ach, wie gar nichts . . .' at b. 105, creating a small a b a complex through the tonal emphasis of G(2) on B♭. The two thoughts of G(3) 'Ach, wie gar nichts . . .' and 'Sie gehen daher . . .' are given two musical ideas, b1 and b2, the second taken over eventually by the choir in frequent repetition, leading to the final questioning on an unresolved diminished chord to the words 'Nun Herr, wess soll ich mich trösten?' This long preparation finds an equally elaborate response in the transition, which is much longer than that in movement 2, nine bars connecting text G(4) 'Ich hoffe auf dich' to text H

'Der Gerechten Seelen . . .'; repetition of the brief text and its phrases are again essential to the great cadence which prepares the pedal fugue, in which text H is constantly repeated.

Movements 1–3: style and expression

The familiarity of the texts which open the *Requiem* finds a natural complement in the musical styles Brahms associates with them: first the alternating statements of a scalar phrase on subdominant and tonic over a pedal (a1); then, in total contrast, the hushed unaccompanied vocal progression in a higher register to the opening words 'Selig sind' (a2): the passage might almost have been written to illustrate the Romantic concept of the 'celestial' quality of a cappella music as opposed to the 'earthly' quality of the instrumental, here associated with the lower strings.[4] Yet the effect does not arise merely from the character of these ideas. The stylistic origin of the opening passage can surely be traced to a familiar archetype of the Lutheran tradition, one made particularly relevant by Brahms's acknowledgement of the presence of a chorale 'in the opening measures':[5] for the passage is effectively a transformation of Baroque chorale-prelude style and could easily be reconstructed to show a complete set of entries of the first chorale phrase in 'pre-imitation' followed by the harmonized chorale in augmented note values. Brahms does not follow this conventional design: rather he places the entire passage over a pedal, gives a skeleton of the harmony instead of the 'first entry', so that the phrase at b. 3 seems to emerge from nothing, extends this 'second entry' into a codetta, then presents, in augmented note values, not the chorale, but a seemingly completely new choral idea a2 (see Example 9).

The choral idea also gives evidence of the importance of distant styles in influencing the work's material. It is immediately notable for its fluid extension and delay of cadential resolution, a process in which a predominance of root-position chords is very conspicuous, giving an archaic sense to the harmony, which is strengthened by the use of unaccompanied voices.[6] The contrast of effect of the second choral theme, b, arises from the regularity of its phrasing and clear harmonic goal-direction through the use of sequence. The agile polyphony into which it resolves shows the instrumental dimension of Brahms's vocal writing, here already prominent before the first overt fugal passage, in the second movement. It is another striking feature to distinguish his choral style from that of his contemporaries, and connect it more directly with that of J. S. Bach.[7]

Like the opening of the first movement, that of the second does not immedi-

Ex. 13 Parallels between Beethoven, Ninth Symphony (Finale) and *Requiem*, movement 2

ately disclose a distant historical origin. The relentless tread of the march, its blunt statement of melody at unison and octave, rising to shattering force with full orchestra and choir, seems a nineteenth-century conception – almost looking towards Mahler in its expressionistic intensity. Yet Brahms identified his theme as a Lutheran chorale melody. The parallels already drawn with the treatment of the first phrase of the chorale in Bach's Cantata 27 ('Wer weiß, wie nahe mir mein Ende') naturally suggest a common background: a chorale fantasia with the introduction serving as ritornello between the successive phrases. Though the process is not taken as far by Brahms – his 'chorale' is of four unequal phrases stated continuously without interlude – the larger-scale effect of the alternation of choral and orchestral material is analogous.[8] As in the first movement, there is a stylistic contrast between orchestral and choral elements. The high-lying, four-part diatonic idiom of the 'trio' 'So seid nun geduldig . . .' resembles other Brahms unaccompanied works in emulation of German Renaissance choral style (notably the *Marienlieder*, Op. 22),[9] though one given a much greater sense of harmonic direction through its sequential writing and regular phrasing.

The arresting choral progression to text E 'Aber des Herrn Wort bleibet in Ewigkeit' represents the first really dramatic, as opposed to forceful, moment in the work so far. Its stark juxtaposed triads, responding syncopated strings and pre-sounding of the fugue subject in the brass build a stylistic bridge to a much more modern vocal style; for the 'fugue subject', 'Die Erlöseten des Herrn . . .', with its strongly defined rhythmic articulation of a chordal shape and distinctive leaping octave finds a parallel not so much in Bach's choral writing as in that of Beethoven (compare the fugal figure at bb. 76–92 of the 'Allegro energico, sempre ben marcato' of the finale of the Ninth Symphony to the words 'Ihr stürzt nieder, Millionen?'). He makes further dramatic use of counterpoint in the central section where the words 'Freude and Wonne' combine the 'original' and augmented version of the same idea, though this is immediately contrasted with chromatically shifting harmony and suddenly reduced dynamics to the words 'und Schmerz und Seufzen', followed by dramatically rising syncopations against the orchestra for the continuation 'wird weg müssen': the latter passage provides a rare example of straightforward word-painting. The recapitulation is signalled in the stretto of the first theme, though the pedal coda treats the imitation of phrases very freely.[10]

The presence of the solo voice in the third movement, declaiming almost unannounced the psalmist's text 'Herr, lehre doch mich . . .', extends the stylistic range more fully up to Brahms's own time. The fusing of recitative and aria into a flexible arioso idiom had been a preoccupation of composers throughout the nineteenth century, especially in opera. The dissolving of formal boundaries was no less important for Brahms in the sphere of choral/orchestral music with solos, with its need for a vocal idiom that could be adapted equally to passages of high intensity and quiet reflection in close association with the choir. However, the stimulus came not from other composers, but rather from Brahms's own songs. A clear precedent can be found in his Op. 32, Nos. 1 and 2, both of which relate to the *Requiem* movement in the sentiment of their texts as well as in musical idiom:[11] the conclusion of each verse and the piano codetta of No. 1 are strikingly like the end of the first section of the third movement, while the arioso-like style of No. 2 clearly anticipates the third movement's general style. An essential feature of the more extended *Requiem* movement is the more fluid character of the harmony. The hesitancy expressed in the text is reflected in a harmonic style in which emphasis is removed from the tonic, the music rather moving around it with an initial minor chord on the 'dominant' (v) and characteristic stress on VI and III: the minor third of v facilitates a melody, the scale of which (D to D with C) might be seen as of 'Dorian' modal character, if it were not so clearly determined by harmony. When the choir repeats the idea, first tentatively, then in all four parts, the idiom takes on yet another aspect, its steady crotchet pulse, underpinned with string pizzicato, creating a distinctive animated march style that moves questioningly forward.

The second section (a1 var) is destined for more dramatic treatment in reflection of its text. The vocal line to text G(3) 'Ach, wie gar nichts . . .' is now more wide-ranging and in higher register. After its initial affirmation of D major, it shifts back to D minor for 'Sie gehen daher wie ein Schemen', initiating a progression of increasing intensity in which the decorative figure of idea b2 is used repeatedly until all the vocal parts coalesce on a questioning dimin-

Movement 3, bb 1-5

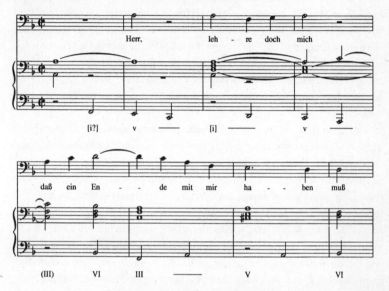

Ex. 14   Movement 3: opening harmonic progression

ished chord to the words 'Nun Herr, wess soll ich mich trösten?' with all the woodwind in triplet chording diminishing to *pp*. This striking moment surely draws even more obviously on the precedent of the finale of Beethoven's Ninth Symphony (compare the 'Adagio ma non troppo, ma divito' bb. 56–60), as does its resolution, the cross rhythms clearly recalling the final cadence for the soloists before the choral/orchestral coda (bb. 836–42).

But this background influence does not inhibit Brahms's treatment of the cadence in its structural context. The even larger cross rhythm through which he creates a very broad hemiola pattern (two bars of 3/4 becoming one of 3/2 in bb. 171–2) produces a cadence which, though influenced by Baroque precedent, is in its effect completely specific to this structural moment, holding back the resolution into the fugue, the entry of which then releases the pent-up expectation. This fugue is certainly the most controversial passage of the work. It represents a bold concept, with the same text repeated in choral entries with increasing levels of dissonance against the bass pedal, a device which symbolizes the security against harm expressed in the text 'Der Gerechten Seelen sind in Gottes Hand'. After the exposition (alternating tonic and dominant entries) the intervals are treated more freely and the subject extended, with a distinctive melismatic quaver figure in the sopranos and more demanding writing for sopranos and tenors (including a high B♭ at b. 190). Finally, paired stretto in bass/tenor and alto/soprano from b. 196 signals the concluding section, with the tenors now assuming the quaver figure and the counterpoint gradually coalescing into the cadence with an overwhelming sense of finality. A major contributor to the sheer energy and fullness of the whole is the orchestra, which conducts an independent four-part fugue on a diminished variant of the choral fugue subject.

The close relation between and frequent interchangeability of choral and orchestral idioms reflects not merely Brahms's structural inclinations but also the music which influenced him, for example the instrumental polyphony of Bach and the homophonic idioms of Schütz and Giovanni Gabrieli. Against this background, the idiomatic use of instruments stands out, for example the introduction of the harp in the second section of the first movement and the role of the flutes in its coda, which play a vital role in achieving a completely new colouring in association with the descending variant of the 'Selig' figure. But the orchestra also has a role in conceiving a sound-world for each movement as a whole. It is crucial to the effect of the opening, where it completely transforms the chorale-prelude idiom by using a rich lower register, with cellos divisi in three, the bottom part doubling the string bass, and with no violins, violas taking the highest part.[12] In the second movement the transformation of a historical model is even more striking; the orchestral march is given a veiled quality at the outset through the division of the violins and violas into a total of six parts, muted, doubled in the wind, including piccolo, with harps, a sound which takes on an entirely different character when the music is played *ff* with strident brass chording. In the third movement the orchestra plays a more dramatic role, in the accompaniment of the solo voice and framing of its appearances. From the very outset, the low-lying horns, divisi violas and cellos, timpani and pizzicato bass perfectly complement the questioning words of the baritone and the shifting harmony, and the open notes of the trumpets and horns intensify the bleakness when the words are taken up by the choir. The effect becomes even more stark when this passage returns to conclude the first section at b. 66, the onward movement frozen in the brass, and the pizzicato strings focusing all attention on the repeated words 'Herr, lehre doch mich . . .' The massive orchestral outburst which concludes this section at b. 93 to the music of 'Siehe, meine Tage . . .' points again to the spirit of Beethoven; it might well be a remnant from the Sonata/Symphony in D minor which Brahms worked on in 1854, stark, massive, and dying away to nothing.[13]

Movements 4–5: textual and musical structure

The central movements of the work stand apart from those which precede and follow them not merely in the predominantly contemplative qualities of their texts, but also in the relation achieved between text and music. The relative lack of internal textual contrast stimulates formal designs which are very different from those of movements 1–3. The form of movement 4 can be seen as the most purely 'musical' of the work, one driven by instrumental processes rather than by the needs of the text (though these are accommodated with an effectiveness which has made it the best-known movement of the work). How one describes this form, however, is by no means obvious. Like that of the first movement, it can be interpreted in more than one way, here as three possible designs creating a reinforcement of the sentiment of the opening text I(1) 'Wie lieblich sind deine Wohnungen': (1) a sonata-style movement with transition to a second subject area, conflated recapitulation and development, and final coda; (2) a ternary form A B A; (3) a broad reprise form A, A1 with coda.

Movement 4

Text	I(1)	I(2)	I(3)	I(1)		I(4)	
Form 1	Ia	tr	II	Ia	Ib tr	Ic dev	I coda
Form 2	A			B			A
Form 3	A			A1			A
Key: E♭	I	I	V	I	mod		I
Bars	1	46	65	89	111	123	154

It fits none of the three precisely. There is considerable precedent in Brahms's instrumental forms for a sonata structure with 'conflated' development and recapitulation (in which the recapitulation of the first subject in the home key occurs before the development, which then leads to the recapitulation of the second subject and concluding material in the home key): however, in this case the second subject never recurs after the imitative passage to text I(3) which can be seen as the 'development' (bb. 123–54). It might be seen as a ternary form, A B A, but the return of the first section to the opening text I(1) (bb. 154–73) is much too abbreviated and tonally conclusive to be seen as balancing the first section. As a reprise form, A A1, the two sections differ too much to be seen as fully related, since the 'development' (bb. 123–54) in A1 effectively supplants the 'second subject and closing group' in A (bb. 65–89). That the spirit of the movement is closest to that of a sonata form is suggested by the instrumental character of the material and its very overt development, which has no parallel in the work (apart from the fugal sections in Nos. 2, 3 and 6, which are specifically devoted to fugal device as a means of conclusion). The numerous repetitions of text-phrases (which occur more pervasively than in any other movement) show textual structure to be subservient to musical considerations. The very sequence of the text is displaced in order to save its one small dynamic contrast (the more animated I(4) 'die loben dich immerdar') for the 'development' section: text I(1) is recalled prior to this with idea 1a in the tonic to give the effect of a reprise or recapitulation, and it recurs at the end of the movement to function as a coda, again with much repetition of the opening phrase 'Wie lieblich . . .' accommodating itself memorably to the cadential needs of the music (bb. 154–66).

The formal structure of movement 5 is very simple by comparison. Though the mood of the text is contemplative throughout, it does include sufficient contrast to be reflected musically in a middle section defined by key and theme, followed by a varied reprise of the first text and music to make a clear A B A form.

Movement 5

Text	J/L	K	J/L
Form	A	B	A
Key: G	I	♭III (mod)	I
bars	1	27	49

Within this simple scheme, however, Brahms introduces an entirely new dimension to the use of text repetition, not merely with short phrases within the solo line (which does much to create its intimate, reflective quality) but by the use of text L sung by the choir, which is closely related to text K given to the soloist. This feature anticipates the parallel which will emerge between movements 7 and 1, but here the musical treatment is more complex, as the soloist's line 'Ich will euch wieder sehen' is accompanied by the choral line 'Ich will euch trösten . . .' in augmentation, a relation emphasized by the fact that the solo line has also been used in the orchestral introduction to open the movement. It is significant that Brahms gives to the choir the text which brings the most intimate consolation in the work, creating a more universal sense of assurance and avoiding the more obvious association of 'a mother' with the solo soprano voice.

Movements 4–5: style and expression

Not only in their sentiments but in their musical styles, movements 4 and 5 stand apart from the norms established in movements 1–3 and reworked and complemented in movements 6–7. For the choral reflection on the eternal bliss

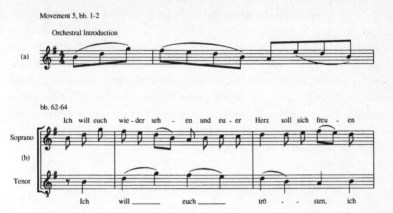

Ex. 15 Movement 5: textual/musical parallels in bb. 1–2 and bb. 62–4

of the courts of the Lord in movement 4, Brahms employs his most accessible idiom: a gentle intermezzo in triple time, major key, which has obvious links with the vocal/instrumental waltzes. That Brahms chose such a popular and secular idiom for the centre of a religious work need cause no surprise, since some of his most sublime effects in the instrumental works arise through the transformation of waltz and dance rhythms generally: one can well conclude that, for him, the contemplation of paradise from an earthly perspective could best be expressed in such music.

The style of the fifth movement is altogether less familiar in Brahms's output. He selects for the most intimate of his texts a movement without any precedent in his vocal works. If the baritone aria of the third movement evolved from the solo songs, this soprano movement has no such obvious origin for its slow and high-lying melismatic solo line, which comes closer to a reflective aria than to a freely-evolving arioso; the orchestral introduction and its careful preparation of the solo entry are also aria-like. However, the idiom remains close to the instrumental sphere, as is shown by the oboe counterpoint to the solo voice and initial apportioning of the vocal melody to the solo cello at the point of recapitulation.[14]

Distinctive orchestration helps to give the fourth movement the feeling of a transformed dance. After the thick doublings of the fugue of the third movement, there here appears soft woodwind colour in the orchestral introduction and especially the coda, alternating with the vocal parts, and a notable use of pizzicato in the strings to suggest the effect of harps, presumably to evoke 'heavenly harps' in contrast to the earthly harps of the orchestra in movements

1, 2 and 7. A particularly apt instrumental feature is the horn arpeggio at the cadence prior to the development (bb. 89–90), further pointing up the movement's instrumental character. In the fifth movement the 'aria', with its supporting flute, oboe and clarinet counterpoint and its delicate halo of muted strings around the soprano part, reveals a pure enjoyment of sound which has no parallel in the work. Perhaps the most striking sonic feature of the movement is the final cadence, almost impressionistic in the way its instrumental voices slowly unfold and coalesce with string harmonics on the final chord, as if to create as detached and ethereal an effect as possible.

Movements 6–7: textual and musical structure

The function of movements 6 and 7 in complementing 1–3 in the total conception (with movement 1 bearing a literal relationship to 7) places special structural weight on movement 6. For this Brahms selects his longest and most varied text and composes his most dramatic and concentrated music. It has clear textual/musical parallels with movement 3, both having a large A B design in which A incorporates extensive solo and choral writing and B is fugal. But the more insistent text of movement 6 prompts a more sectionalized form, with A divided into two much more distinct parts than in movement 3 (and without the need of its inner reprise). The solo/choral relation is now confined almost entirely to the first part (a2) to enable a self-contained 'Vivace' for chorus (a2) to focus on the prophecy of the day of judgement (with only passing participation by the soloist). The concluding fugue (c) in major mode is much more lengthy and developed than the parallel sections of movements 2 and 3, in accordance with its function of establishing the work's long-term structural dominant.

Movement 6

Text	M	N(1)	N(2)	N(3)	N(4)	N(3)	O(1)	O(2)	O(1)	O(2)	O(1)	O(2)	O(1)
Form 1	A						B						
Form 2	a1 (ch)	a2 (s/ch)	(tr)	b	(a2)	b	c1	c2	c1	c2	c1	c2	c1
Key: c:C	i(V)	i(V) mod	♭II–V	i	i mod	i mod	I	V mod	(I)	I	(I)	(I)	I
Bars	1	28	68	82	109	127	208	234	248	290	304	316	330

The communal voice of Text M 'Denn wir haben hie keine bleibende Statt' determines the choral opening of this movement; the words are partially repeated for emphasis and to make the first important musical cadence. The solo voice follows announcing the prophecy 'Siehe, ich sage euch ein Geheimnis' N(1), the successive lines of which are repeated by the choir: 'Wir werden nicht immer schlafen alle entschlafen, wir werden aber alle verwandelt werden . . . zu der Zeit der letzten Posaune'; the latter words N(2) are repeated by chorus and orchestra to make the major cadence which finally clinches the long-suspended dominant of the movement as the uncertainty of the text is resolved into the assurance of the prophecy.

Now, at the climax of the prophecy, the text 'Denn es wird die Posaune schallen' N(3) is given central focus by being placed into a much tighter rhythmic setting. Taking his cue from the rhythmic parallel between the lines 'Denn es wird die Posaune schallen' and 'Der Tod ist verschlungen in den Sieg', Brahms designs one musical strophe for the three lines of text beginning with these words, the third line extended by repetition to give emphasis and to complete the musical cadence. The intensified effect of the second strophe arises not only from the textual and musical anacrusis ('Der/Tod') but from the fact that the solo voice has been recalled to the music of bb. 28–32 to sing the intervening text N(4) 'Dann, dann wird erfüllet werden das Wort, das geschrieben steht', a striking moment in which the composer further intensifies the contrast between the announcement of prophecy by the soloist and the delivery of its substance by the choir. From this point onwards the increasing use of sequence in the music as it moves towards the climax of the passage involves more textual repetition. But Brahms adjusts the succession of musical ideas to enhance the final cadence. He now avoids reflecting the obvious rhetorical parallel between the words 'Tod, wo ist dein Stachel?' and 'Hölle, wo ist dein Sieg?' In order to expand the development to the climax by having two ideas for these texts, he treats the first text in sequence (bb. 152–8) then generates a new figure for 'Hölle, wo ist dein Sieg?', repeated in sequence (bb. 159–67), enabling both to return at the climax, the latter with a yet more intensified figure leading to the emphatic final cadence 'Wo, wo, wo ist dein Sieg?' The great sense of expansiveness in the fugue which follows results from both length (bb. 209–349) and structure. The length inevitably involves textual repetition. But Brahms associates repetition with musical processes as well as themes, so that music and text are one as the structure gradually accumulates its weight and drama. The two chief textual ideas provide the musical ideas: 'Herr, du bist würdig zu nehmen Preis und Ehre und Kraft' (O1) the fugue subject (c1), and 'denn du hast alle Dinge geschaffen und durch deinen Willen haben sie das Wesen und sind geschaffen' (O2) a totally contrasted lyrical idea (c2) (its two phrases fall into yet further distinct ideas – homophonic then imitative, the latter facilitating the return of the fugue subject at b. 244). Though the regular exposition of the fugue subject suggests that text will be allocated successively to musical subjects, the text/music relation is soon turned to more dramatic purposes. The returning subject heralds an emphatic repetition of the second phrase of the first line 'zu nehmen Preis und Ehre', which now assumes greater importance than the first phrase, as its own segment of the fugue subject becomes used as an independent figure in modulating sequence; in turn, the repetition of the opening text and subject gives added force to the repetition of the second phrase in making the first of two major cadences at a remove from the tonic at b. 289 (on D major as V of V). This weighty climax acts as a foil to the return of text O(2), its lyrical music now given more repetition and a new and more intense musical shape before the stretto of the first subject hurls the choral mass towards a second major cadence, now at two further dominant removes at b. 315 (E major as V/V/V of V); from this point the lyrical theme to text O(2) again works its way back to a stretto on the first subject proper (O(1)) and a massive homophonic conclusion. Much of the force of the two major cadences arises from the fact that the fugue subject almost always reappears in the tonic after episodes, this constant reference surely mirroring the text's expression of the authority of God.

Movement 7 has to perform two functions within the larger structure: to bring about tonal resolution and balance the great weight of movement 6, and to conclude the work as a whole. It is a special feature of the *Requiem* that Brahms does the latter by revealing through the same music the unity of the parallel texts A/B and P. He uses two different types of music to text P. The first setting disposes the two lines P(1) and P(2) in a ternary form a b a; the second recalls only P(1) to the music of the first movement. The form of a is the most straightforward after that of the funeral march of the second movement. In view of its brevity the text requires a great deal of repetition, but the structural relationship between text and music is still retained by setting its two thoughts to different music. First the whole of P(2) 'Ja der Geist spricht, daß sie ruhen von ihrer Arbeit' is used as a transition from a to b; but the second part, b, is largely based only on its second phrase 'daß sie ruhen von ihrer Arbeit' which thus emerges with special force. The second setting uses only the first line P(1).

Movement 7

Text	P(1)	P2(1/2)	P2(2)	P(2)[1]		[2]	P(1)		P(1)	P(1)
Form 1	A								B	
Form 2	a		tr	b	tr	b	a	tr	[1/a2]	
Key F	I	V	V–III	III	V of III mod	III	I		♭VII/mod	I
Bars	1	34	40	47	76	88	102	131	132	147

The use of the brief text P1 for the whole of section a enables the music to achieve a more purely musical elaboration than at any point since movement 4. With no internal contrasts, it inexorably unfolds a broad musical exposition

Movement 7, bb. 1-5

Movement 7, bb. 24-27

Ex. 16 Movement 7: harmonic parallels with movement 1

and transition to the dominant key with brief orchestral introduction and more lengthy coda. It clearly alludes to the first movement in both thematic and harmonic terms. The great subject given by sopranos to 'Selig sind die Toten' unites two versions of the basic 'Selig' figure of the work as well as alluding to the particular descending version of the coda of the first movement which will finally return as the coda to the work. In harmonic terms, its initial tonic prolongation is closely related to the opening progression of the first movement (Example 16; cf. Example 9). Additionally, the unfolding of the transition from tonic to dominant seems to recall the alternative key centre of the first movement, D♭, in its Neapolitan inflection of the progression to the dominant of F (bb. 24–7 of movement 7; Example 16).

Textual repetition is just as important in the second section b. After the use of the whole text as a transition, this section picks up the second phrase 'daß sie ruhen von ihrer Arbeit', which is presented twice, the second a variant of the first, ending with repetition of the final line. The entire text and music are now repeated with elaboration of the transition material in the dominant of A major before the second line again takes precedence with repetition, ending with an enhanced cadence on the dominant of A. The return of the A section of the movement is considerably abbreviated before the sudden transition to the reprise of the first movement material to the text of the first line 'Selig sind die Toten'.

Brahms can now re-set the opening words of movement 7 to the music of the first movement because of the comparable syllabic structure of the respective lines ('Selig sind, die da Leid tragen' / 'Selig sind die Toten, die in den Herrn sterben'). Having established the material of the first movement (1: a2) he is now in a position to unveil the relationship not only between the text and music of movements 1 and 7 (coda), but also the first part of movement 7. As he introduces the descending variant of the 'Selig' figure in the woodwind during the retransition to the tonic (bb. 136–7), so its relation to the passage just completed to this text becomes clear. When this figure becomes pervasive to the text 'Selig sind' in the final passage of the movement (beginning b. 151) it makes a direct link to the parallel passage of the first movement, where its text is 'getröstet werden', thus more deeply uniting the texts of the first and last movements. The emphasis on these words through choral imitation, and the fact that the work ends with the word 'Selig', rather than completing the line '. . . sind die Toten, die in den Herrn sterben' makes a link to the very opening choral words and finally impresses on the listener the core sentiment: the assurance of a state of blessedness.

Movements 6–7: style and expression

Conspicuous stylistic features of movements 6 and 7 complement those of movements 1–3 in the large-scale process of retransition towards the recapitulated material in the latter part of movement 7. The opening choral march of movement 6 'Denn wir haben hie . . .' is closely akin to the choral version of 'Herr, lehre doch mich' in movement 3. And harmony is again the conspicuous means of textual expression both here and throughout the movement. The more insistent character of the music results in the suspension of the tonic chord through the first section, which is entirely in the dominant region, G (though its ultimate context is never lost sight of in the opening harmonic progression V–ii–V–i–V), with a notable emphasis on VI (see Example 17 for a summary of the tonal pattern of the entire movement).

But this is to be a more dramatic movement than No. 3, as the bold modulation to A minor at b. 9 within the suspended C minor passage intimates. So does the more open character of the recitative by which means the soloist enters with the announcement of the prophecy at b. 28: this is the most obvious use of the style so far. But the recitative also serves a structural function as transition to a new key, as Brahms draws again on the distinctive E♭6 chord of the opening progression (b. 4) to make a modulation to D♭ minor (enharmonically notated as C♯ minor) as a musical expression of the revelation of the mystery of transformation (with a conspicuous melisma on the word 'Geheimnis' as well). The revelation is now given out in successive lines by soloist repeated almost on a monotone by chorus. These statements are now far from the tonic (in F♯ minor and C♯ minor). With the sudden end of the text 'Wir werden aber alle verwandelt werden . . . in einem Augenblick' a more dramatic recitative style appears in the solo part, echoed by the choir, stamping out the words 'zu der Zeit der letzten Posaune', with trombone and tuba chords taken over by the choir and orchestra as a musical transition to the 'Vivace' which follows. But, as in the preceding passage of recitative, a structural function is more important than the illustrative. The brass/choral calls serve the double function of recitative/musical symbol and structural transition. It is in the 'Vivace' that the real resolution comes, and Brahms gives this his fullest musical treatment. Thus he ignores the approach taken by those composers, for example Mozart, Berlioz and Verdi, who express the imagery of the analogous text in the Latin Requiem Mass ('Tuba mirum') in extensive fanfare passages.

The massive effect of the 'Vivace' arises from its elemental musical character and dramatic use of tonality. In stylistic terms, this is a vastly quickened and more impetuous version of the triple-time 'march' of the second movement, and it also resolves the thematically (and textually) related passage which precedes it (see Example 4 for the related variants of the chorale source). So characteristic of Brahms is the 'Vivace' that it clearly became an archetype of expression for him: he draws on a very similar idiom for the central section of the *Schicksalslied* ('Allegro', also C minor, 3/4), where it again represents a picture of the fall of man into the abyss, with rapidly running orchestral basses, tremolando strings, choral syncopations and reiterated phrases.[15] The close relation of the 'Vivace' to the preceding passage is shown in several other ways. First, with the recall of the solo voice for the 'recitative' passage of the text, the music returns at the same pitch, though now firmly resolved in the tonic, thus tying the text and music of the sections more fully together. Second, the 'development' towards the climax mirrors the chromatic sequence of the fanfares through C♯ major, D major and E♭ major. Finally, the preparation for the clinching cadence to the section is dramatically enhanced by the placement of the chord of E major within the sequence (iv–♭ii[Np]–♯III–V–I). This appears as a culmination of a relationship which has been gradually unveiled through the movement (G/e, c/e, c/E) and will have yet a further role in the fugue by the juxtaposition of C/E and cadential repetition to sectionalize the text.

Just as the 'Vivace' resolves the textual and tonal uncertainty of the first part of the movement, so it too is destined for a yet greater resolution from minor to

Movement 6

Ex. 17 Movement 6: tonal outlines of the 'Andante' and 'Vivace'; cadential
progression at the end of the 'Vivace'

major and into a mood of unreserved rejoicing expressed in its very grandly
planned fugue 'Herr, du bist würdig'. The effect also arises from the nature of
the subject itself, solid and instrumental, in the *organo pleno* tradition of the
organ fugues of Bach (or of Mendelssohn emulating Bach). As in movements 2
and 3, the power of the fugal entry is enhanced by the preparation of the
cadence. The Vivace ends on a very long-held major chord with running bass,
the end of which reveals the fugue subject in the tenor with extraordinarily
dramatic effect.[16] However, Brahms transcends his instrumental precedent by
the length and structural scope of the fugue which follows. This is especially
the result of the contrasted theme to text O(2), an idea which is very flexible
and which is played against the main theme in the tonic. At its first appearance
it possesses a remarkable fluidity, first motivic in character and modulating
quickly, then developing into a lyrical imitative figure which can exist on its
own yet also relate to the main figure by use of a shared counter-subject. (It
seems to mediate between the spirit of the *Liebeslieder Waltzes* and fugal
idiom.)

In achieving the transition from the climax of movement 6 in a now totally
secure C major to the reprise of movement 1, Brahms opts for an idiom and
formal design previously unhinted at in his work and specific to this particular

Movement 7

Bach: St Matthew Passion No 29 'O Mensch, bewein...'

Ex. 18 Movement 7: parallels in figuration with Bach, *St Matthew Passion*

text. In movement 7, the first part of the A section carries the designation 'Feierlich' ('In Ceremonial Style'), a term with particularly strong Schumann associations: Schumann uses it for two of the movements of his own Requiem Mass (to Latin texts) and also when evoking the image of a 'solemn ceremony' in the fourth movement of the *Rhenish Symphony*.[17] All are stately movements in common time. Brahms's movement, more than any other part of the work, certainly conveys the sense of a 'solemn ceremony' filling the spaces of a great ecclesiastical building. The effect comes from the great breadth of the musical structure (the harmony gradually unfolding the tonic before moving towards the dominant) as well as from other specific musical techniques. The idiom might at first appear to be that of an accompanied fugue, with tonic and dominant entries in soprano and bass. But there is no counter-subject and the second entry subtly modifies the subject, which is freely elaborated from the third entry in all parts. Viewed more broadly, the passage can be seen as complementing the first part of the first movement in the transformation of a traditional device to new expressive purposes. Indeed the omnipresent appoggiatura phrasing in the orchestral strings is very reminiscent of the chorale fantasia which closes Part I of Bach's *St Matthew Passion* (compare also the active bass line in contrary motion with the upper part).[18] But before the presentation of P2 to music b, Brahms builds a much greater contrast into the movement than had appeared in the first movement. After the first section has ended with a codetta on the dominant, with typically Brahmsian cross rhythms and pizzicato conclusion, a much more distant idiom appears, intensifying the almost ecclesiastical mood of the preceding section. Like a voice from eternity, the choir intones the assurance of eternal rest to the words 'Ja der Geist spricht, daß sie ruhen von ihrer Arbeit', accompanied by trombone and horn chorus. This is the most overtly archaic moment in the work, recalling seven-teenth-century music for choir and brass such as that in Schütz's *Symphoniae Sacrae*.[19] Yet the archaism is only one side of the stylistic extremes which give it such striking and cumulative effect, for the second phrase of the second line 'daß sie ruhen von ihrer Arbeit' is given the greatest expressive contrast within any one movement. At the promise of eternal rest the music opens up into the key of A major in rich lyrical phrases supported by pizzicato lower strings in triplets. The tonal contrast of F major to A major mirrors that of F major to D♭ in the first movement: the sentiment of travail and sadness which is expressed in the contrast with the flat-side lower key is now transformed to that of secure rest and reward in the bright relationship to the upper mediant major key, A. This passage delays its conclusion by interrupted cadences which give the impression that the composer can hardly bring himself to dispel the mood before the return to the A section, where the vocal scoring is varied.

The great effect of the subsequent return of the opening material of the work is created by a number of features, uniting the formal and expressive dimensions. When the music of the first movement returns through an inter-rupted cadence to E♭, this appears as a continuation of a series of interrupted cadences and unexpected modulations in the latter part of the B section and notably in the return of the A section. The use of E♭ for music originally associ-ated with F places a clear emphasis on this key, which lies most distant from the tonic in the work's tonal plan (and offers the greatest clash in the sequence of movements, d/E♭ between movements 3 and 4). The second stage of the retransition is to D♭, the contrasted key of the first movement, which had like-wise first appeared by a semitonal clash C/D♭ without preparation. Thus Brahms surveys important key contrasts of the work in the process of effec-tively re-establishing the tonic with ultimate security for the last words of the text.

Though the music of the first movement coda is recalled with relatively little adjustment, orchestration does play a crucial role in transforming its effect. But before this takes place, the scoring of movement 6 serves a different purpose, geared to predominantly choral effects with less room for instrumen-tal features. However, the role of the orchestra is very telling. In the opening antiphonal call between strings and woodwind, a feature which continues through the first section, it seems to act like a guide to the chorus, pointing the way through the first section, supported by pizzicato strings to give an added sense of onward movement. After the entry of the baritone, the strings and woodwind enable the vocal theme to be carried in the orchestra while the chorus sing the text on a monotone, thus greatly enhancing its effect through understatement. At the transition Brahms takes the text almost literally: 'der letzten Posaune' becomes three trombones and a tuba in heavy chording. The 'Vivace' itself gains added effect from the use of the piccolo (for the only time in the work, save the second movement) as well as the agitated string writing. As in the fugue of movement 3, the independent orchestral counter-subject adds greatly to the fullness of the effect, though the strings also have a lyrical role, contrasting with the massive force of the full orchestra in the final cadence.

Section A of movement 7 also derives its sense of breadth from orchestral figuration: the high exposed soprano line is only fully effective because of the active string phrasing from the bass upwards, providing an essential complement which could not be produced vocally. The following transition passage takes almost all its effect from the timbre and pitch of the trombones and blending horns, which create a sense both of the distance Brahms required for his text and, through their liturgical associations in choral music, of timelessness with a religious context. There could be no greater contrast than with the expressive wind phrases and sextuplet figuration in the strings which follow, and which throw such a different emphasis on the words. In the final process of retransition to the music of the first movement, it is the association of the descending variant of the 'Selig' figure in the woodwind which first draws the listener's attention to its significance. And as the music modulates through to its final resolution, the effect is intensified as the idea appears in all the wind voices, most notably in the high flute at bb. 143–5, which most closely anticipates the closing choral imitation of 'Selig sind' and casts a special aura of peace over the final bars.

4

Reception

Early performances

When the first three movements of the *Requiem* had their premiere in Vienna on 1 December 1867, the name of Brahms would have been associated by his audience with his performances of Baroque choral works with the Wiener Singverein in the season 1863–4: a largely unknown repertoire received with considerable reserve. He could now expect a similar response towards his own music, which shared many of the same influences. This was obviously the assumption of the conductor, Johann Herbeck, who, as the record of the event states, 'really knew the character of his public well' and found a complete performance of the 'just as often serious as extensive composition' risky, obtaining Brahms's consent to give a partial one.[1] Moreover, despite the status of conductor and performers, the performance was not faultless. Although the first two movements caused no adverse comment, the third movement became notorious because the percussionist in the concluding pedal fugue ('Der Gerechten Seelen sind in Gottes Hand . . .') misunderstood Brahms's marking *fp* and played *f* and even apparently *ff* throughout, drowning out the other parts. The débâcle naturally added to the controversy by now expected to attend any new work by Brahms in Vienna. On the side of his supporters was Vienna's leading music critic, Eduard Hanslick of the *Neue freie Presse*. But even he had his reservations: first, that the work was not ideally suited to a concert room (which echoes his responses to Brahms's performances with the Singverein) and second, that its character imposed limitations on ready acceptance: 'It is understandable that a composition so difficult to grasp, and which deals only with ideas of death, cannot anticipate popular success and will be uncongenial to many elements of the broader public.'[2] But he immediately grasped its power and significance, taking offence at the manner of the opposition in the audience (though this was apparently more from 'conservatives' than New Germans), commenting 'we should have supposed . . . that a sense of the greatness and seriousness of the work would have suggested itself even to those who do not like it, and would have won their respect. This seems not to have been the case with a dozen grey-haired fanatics of the old school who had the rudeness to greet the applauding majority and the composer as he appeared with prolonged hissing.' Hanslick placed the work in the broadest historical perspective in the course of a lengthy review:

The Geman Requiem is a work of unusual significance and great mastery. It seems to us one of the ripest fruits to have emerged from the style of the late Beethoven in the field of sacred music. Since the masses for the dead and mourning cantatas of our classical composers the shadow of death and the seriousness of loss have scarcely been presented in music with such power. The harmonic and contrapuntal art which Brahms learnt in the school of Bach and is inspired by him with the living breath of the present, almost recedes for the listener behind the mounting expression from touching lament to anni-hilating death-shudder.[3]

The incumbent of Hanslick's previous post at *Die Presse*, Karl Schelle, earlier inclined to Brahms, was less enthusiastic. After reviewing the first number sympathetically and the second almost so, he concludes 'unfortunately the third is extremely inferior[to movement 2]. The text demanded a strong increase of effect which the composer has been incapable of giving. The bass solo is not written gratefully for the voice and there is much that is obtrusively bizarre and unedifying in the chorus . . . The movement was a failure.'[4] Brahms could expect much less support from the Wagnerian camp. Hirsch, of the *Wiener Zeitung*, grasped the opportunity for criticism, speaking of the 'heathenish noise' of the percussion and asserting 'in the interest of truth' that the opposition party had 'an immense majority'.[5] Of Brahms's close circle, Joachim naturally played down the disturbance, though he also admitted the limitations of the performance. He wrote to his wife immediately after the performance 'I have had my only absolute plea-sure, when the three first movements of Brahms's Requiem were played, although imperfectly . . . who knows how long Brahms will have to wait before he hears it played as it ought to be played. The audience listened sym-pathetically. A compact little party showed reverence and *enthusiasm*. A few cads who hissed met with no success. Brahms was loudly called for.'[6] Another perspective on the Viennese audience comes from Brahms's new and very close friend, the leading surgeon and amateur musician Theodor Billroth, whose critical view of music, including that of Brahms, makes his frankness the more valuable. 'Hanslick says, quite rightly, that [Brahms] has the same fault as Bach and Beethoven; too little of the sensuous in his art both as com-poser and pianist. I think it is as much an intentional avoidance of everything sensuous as it is a fault. His Requiem is nobly spiritual and so Protestant-Bachish that it was difficult to make it go down here. The hissing and clapping became really violent; it was a party conflict. In the end the applause conquered.'[7]

After these mixed reactions in Vienna, where Brahms was still only slowly establishing himself, his reception in the north German city of Bremen for the first performance on 10 April 1868 was very positive indeed, reflecting both its pride in a major musical event associated with a local composer, and the acknowledgement of the importance of that composer and his work.

This Good Friday's performance will not only be of special significance for Bremen but will arouse great interest in the whole of musical Germany since it is concerned with the first performance of a work whose partial performance several months ago in Vienna drew the widest admiration of friends of music, and whose creator, Herr Johannes Brahms, is generally recognized as one of the most progressive living masters in the field of instrumental music. Fifteen years ago, Robert Schumann predicted for the young man an extraordinary future. But because the fulfilment of such predictions in the achievement of the highest results takes time, Brahms has only moved slowly along this path, like Beethoven limiting himself for long to working on strict chamber music before he presented a great choral work.[8]

The performance lived up to the many expectations.

The Requiem of Brahms is an artistic achievement of great value. In order to be able sufficiently to estimate its worth, one must intimately understand the spirit of Schumann's compositions. Our opinion is that Brahms specifically seeks to develop this spirit, the special inclination of the master. Not that he does not already stand at the highest level, but we have much in him to await. In the Requiem we have nothing to do with outer imitation. Brahms has remained himself throughout, whether in modulation, accent or rhythm . . . In the mastery of form he has reached a level which knows no more difficulties.[9]

Negative comments were few. 'To the dark side belong the too concise and actually ungrateful solos, an often too grey colour in instrumentation, a certain brittleness in the connecting of movements one to another . . . above all a somewhat notable unease in modulation.'[10] The orchestra was regarded as outstanding, not least in the effect of the organ. The exactitude and cleanness of execution was widely recognized. A weakness in the choir was the intonation of the sopranos in high-lying parts and the inadequate balance of choir and orchestra. Stockhausen's indisposition was noted, which may have affected the perception of the difficulties of the solo part. Even the criticism of Brahms's opponents in the *Neue Zeitschrift für Musik* was muted in comparison with the earlier Viennese reviews. 'We take the opportunity to speak of the most significant follower of Schumann . . . for whose striving towards musical achievement we have the greatest respect . . . We have always taken the greatest interest in the young composer . . . However, the work lies rather in the direction of, and shows the nature of, ascetic Christian-German composition, which hinders us in warming towards his inspiration. We hope he will withdraw himself more from this subjectivity in the course of time.'[11] A second performance was arranged at the Bremen Union three weeks later on 24 April, giving the critics the required opportunity for the refinement of their ideas: the impression was equally great.

Following the two Bremen performances, the work was given once more publicly (movements 1, 2, 4 and 6 only) on 16 February at the Gurzenich concerts in Cologne under Ferdinand Hiller. Only two days later it received the premiere of its final seven-movement version at the seventeenth Leipzig Gewandhaus concert under Karl Reinecke. For Brahms, the venue of Leipzig was more problematical than that of Bremen. It had been the location of a disastrous early public performance of his first major work with orchestra, the D minor piano concerto, and its resistance continued with critical reaction to his chamber music. This reserve remained at the first hearing of the *Requiem*. The leading critic of the *Musikalisches Wochenblatt* found it 'too contemplative', observing that Protestant church music of the present day displayed 'powerful, valuable, simple, clear, strongly formed' features but that, in contrast, Brahms's was 'a mystical voice' and that the work displayed weakness in its 'lengths' and 'empty passages'.[12] Against this, however it must be added that the editor of the paper, E. W. Fritzsch, found this criticism superficial and unappreciative and became a strong Brahms supporter in the city.[13] By the time of the second Leipzig performance in 1873, at St Thomas's Church, where J. S. Bach had once been director of music, the work had a much more appreciative reception, and Brahms gained both a place in the musical life of the city and a circle of supporters from this time. During the remaining part of 1869 the Requiem received no less than eleven performances, mainly through professional conductor friends of the composer, some of whom had had a knowledge of the work in progress. The second performance, only a week after that in Leipzig, was in Basel under Ernst Reiters; the third took place in Hamburg, the city of his birth, in the church of Brahms's baptism, the Michaelskirche, under Julius von Bernuth. Hermann Levi directed at Karslruhe, Julius Otto Grimm at Münster, and Friedrich Hegar at Zurich (twice in three days); there were also private performances at Dessau and Weimar. The year 1870 saw the first complete performance in Cologne, now under Friedrich Gernsheim, as well as performances at Dresden, at Oldenburg (under Dietrich), and at Kassel. The many informed critical reactions in Cologne brought a deeper insight into the work and the composer and indicated a great respect for Brahms in the

Rhineland region which had such important associations for him (his connection with Schumann): it was recognized that limitations of the performance
did not reflect on the quality of the work. The year 1871 saw the first complete
Viennese performance on 5 March under Brahms himself at the Gesellschaft
der Musikfreunde, followed by performances at Bremen (also under Brahms)
and again at Cologne (again under Gernsheim). By this stage Brahms's reputation in Vienna had increased greatly and he was about to become director of the
Gesellschaft der Musikfreunde. But Vienna remained a problematic venue for
new music and the reception was cool, May noting that it had 'no striking
success';[14] responses were still influenced by memories of movements 1–3 four
years earlier. Berlin and Munich remained the two principal venues the work
had to conquer. They were not, like Leipzig, to be so easily overcome. The
work was given in Berlin on 26 March 1872 under Holländer with the Cäcilien-
verein, and was repeated by them on 29 November. The performances fuelled
the considerable arguments about Brahms which were not resolved by the time
the First Symphony appeared in 1876. In the Catholic south, the responses of
Munich were seemingly more negative than polemical. Brahms was regarded
as 'scarcely more than a name' by the reviewer of the first performance on 24
March 1872, though he had a great future supporter in its conductor, the
young Franz Wüllner. The work found itself compared with the Requiem of
Franz Lachner.[15]

Technical evaluation

As well as the immediate press reactions to the early performances, there
emerged a more technical response to the work in published form. The two
most extensive accounts are by Adolf Schubring (in the *Allgemeine musikalische
Zeitung* in 1869) and Amadeus Macewski (in the *Musikalisches Wochenblatt* in
1870). Schubring's admiration for Brahms, whom he had followed since his
earliest Hamburg years, comes through clearly in a review with no reservations
(though it also implied that the work would encounter resistance): 'Brahms's
German Requiem will have great success wherever it is given a good performance. It is music of indescribable novelty, strength and freshness, now of
elegiac peace, now of lyric beauty, now convulsively dramatic, the finest contrapuntal art clothed in folk-like style, and with it a harmony and orchestration
as practical and effective as we have hitherto experienced in a work of church
music.'[16] He sees the Requiem in the loftiest line of succession: 'as artful and
serious as Sebastian Bach, as elevated and powerful as Beethoven's *Missa
Solemnis*, and saturated in its melody and harmony by Schubert's benevolent

influence'. He was particularly interested in the new uses to which Brahms put strict traditional compositional devices, most notably counterpoint. His attention was naturally directed to the fugues of movements 2, 3 and 6. In movement 3 he notes that the pedal fugue is built as a double fugue for choir and orchestra and records the number of entries of the vocal subject and of the strettos, identifying them in technical terms as *dux* and *comes*. He rightly describes the fugal section of movement 2 as a fugato rather than a fugue, pointing out the passages of augmentation and diminution and the pedal coda. He interprets the fugue of No. 6 as a triple fugue, again identifying the technical functions of the subjects in the vocal and orchestral parts and showing the derivation of a freer 'third' subject.

In addition to these formal contrapuntal features, he also notes the use of strict devices in 'free' contexts. Movement 5 is regarded as 'almost as artful as lovely'; with 'the deepest, mildest seriousness' combined in the 'finest contrapuntal art', noting again the two main themes of the first part employed in imitation (in augmentation and diminution). In movement 4 he notes the 'free canonic imitation' and a longer canonically controlled middle section in 'three interrupted passages'. In one example from movement 3 he even seeks to show how three thematic elements fit contrapuntally and generate, as a new counterpoint, the following fugue subject (a view from which, however, Brahms demurred in his correspondence with Schubring). Schubring was particularly struck by examples of a synthesis between traditional devices and modern features, which he identified particularly in harmonic terms, as at the beginning of movement 4, commenting that 'this movement begins in a wholly modern way with the dominant seventh chord, through here it is linked to classical counterpoint by the inversion of the introduction'. He seems to have regarded any evidence of an uncertain tonal opening as modern in character. Thus of the opening of the work:

Already in the first bars we are in no doubt that we have a modern work before us [bb. 1–5]. Initially one believes oneself to be on firm ground, but is doubtful as to whether F major or minor will come next. The F in the basses, which seems so secure, now in the second bar becomes the dominant seventh of B♭; in the third bar we are in B♭ major, and in the fourth bar . . . in C minor, until finally in the fifth bar with the complete F major chord [the key of F] is finally confirmed.[17]

Schubring also notes the harmonic ambivalence of the opening of the sixth movement, ascribing the harmony to modal influence in a 'rising C minor scale, plagally inflected, of C, D, E♭, F, G, A, B, C (in this case a melody revolving around the notes G, A, B, C, D, E♭, F, G): a scale in any case very appropriate to an expression of the uncertainty and hesitation of everything mortal'.

But above all, he notes the 'complete integration of the up-to-date content with the most beautiful form, a modern masterwork, as we have long realized'.[18]

Macewski shared Schubring's perspective on the historical lineage of the work from Bach and Beethoven as part of a broader perspective on a modern musical world now dominated by programme music. But though certainly echoing Schubring's observation of Brahms's uses of counterpoint and harmony, and the synthesis of old and new, he lays particular stress on the thematic aspect, especially the 'logical' aspect of the working. He is struck by the nature of Brahmsian melody in the broadest sense, noting its individuality: it is no more melody in the old sense, but organic melody from beginning to end, as in the fourth movement, seen as the 'crown' of the work, a 'masterpiece of charming, flowing melody'.[19] He finds a special form of 'musical logic' in such passages as theme 'b' of movement 1, where he notes the passage of sequence from bb. 47 to 51 observing the inversion of the choral melody in the bass at b. 50. Though he gives little attention to movements 1 and 7, he notes the link between them, pointing to the motive at b. 106 as having a vital role in the reprise in No. 7. In No. 7 itself, the sudden transitional cadence to the coda at b. 96 is also highlighted. Unlike Schubring, Macewski admits to certain weaknesses in the work. For example, in the second movement, the bold harmony of the transitional passage to the words 'Aber des Herrn Wort . . .' is seen as 'vulgar' and the connection to the fugue 'rather lame'. Of the work's orchestration he refers to an 'ascetic modern colouring, for example in the three-part cello division at the opening'.[20]

Though a more complete survey of the many responses to the work shows a wider range of reservation, there was general agreement that the most effective and characteristic movements were 1, 4 and 5: the first and fifth for their rapt spirituality, the fourth for beauty of sound. Movement 6 was generally regarded as the greatest structural achievement. The weight of contrapuntal writing was regarded by some commentators as excessive, and attacked as academic, though many observed the freedom of Brahms's use of strict devices and the transformation of fugal passages by textural and harmonic contrasts. This criticism has remained into the twentieth century: Specht comments of these sections that Brahms 'is less an inventor than a constructor, inclined to choose themes less for their intrinsic value than for the possibilities of their manifold development'.[21] An important criticism of the counterpoint was its effect on the clarity of the text. Some writers found the dramatic choral writing and syncopated rhythm in the fugue of movement 2 at the words 'wird weg müssen' too drastic. The two baritone solos, seen as rather too difficult, were not widely appreciated. Many critics who had found Brahms's earlier music too reflective did not change their opinions with the *Requiem*. However, despite these many caveats and the universal recognition of the work's great difficulty in performance, its importance as a new kind of religious music was immediately grasped by the majority of critics. Thus Kleinert could observe in the *Neue Evangelische Kirchenzeitung* that 'the music of the future, for others a vogue, is for Brahms already a music of the past'.[22]

Opponents, and reactions abroad

In addition to the purely musical dimension of its reception, the dissemination of the *Requiem* coincided with an important phase of German history: the victory of the Prussian armies in the Franco-Prussian war of 1870 and the foundation of the German Empire under Bismarck in 1871. The intensely German quality of Brahms's work inevitably made something of a focus for national feeling at this time and Brahms was very happy for it to be used to commemorate the victory. But by the same token it quickly alienated those who were fundamentally opposed to Brahms's implicit claim to express the spirit of modern German music and regarded him as a reactionary, especially Wagner and his circle. Wagner had admired Brahms's skill in variation composition when they were acquainted in the early 1860s, but the appearance of the *Requiem* helped to change his attitude towards the younger composer drastically. Wagner had already expressed his displeasure at the popularity of the *Triumphlied*, written specifically for the victory of 1870 and completed in the following year, referring contemptuously to Brahms adopting a 'Hallelujah wig', a reference to the Handelian element in the work. But the much more extensive *Requiem* alienated him further. He later commented gratuitously at the end of an article on a completely unrelated topic, that, when the present generation dies, 'we will want no German Requiem to be played to our ashes'.[23]

The Wagnerians now saw the *Requiem* as an embodiment of the Protestant-bourgeois religious ethic in music by which they felt so threatened. It was indeed gaining great support, as the press review of a Karlsruhe performance of the *Triumphlied* in 1872 shows:

To the year 1870 attaches, not only the renown of our arms, but a new epoch in our musical art . . . It is based upon the modern development of long-familiar form and modes of expression. That this development has shown itself to be true and healthy (who had not forseen it in Brahms's German Requiem!) is the merit of the German master Brahms, the greatest of the present day![24]

Such contrasting views were to be slow to merge, and Ochs could still comment around the turn of the century that 'the German Requiem has had to fight rather long for the establishment of its assured place in the artistic world'.[25]

However, in places supportive towards Brahms the new work moved quickly forward. Between 1869 and 1876 there were seventy-nine recorded performances, some far afield.[26] Reception in Catholic countries was inevitably less immediate, though its religious content seems to have interested some French musicians; Franck may well have had it in mind, both for its text and as an example of modern religious music, when composing *Les Béatitudes*.[27] It was given by the pioneering J. E. Pasdeloup in his *Concerts populaires* on Good Friday 1875,[28] though this was a feeble performance and the work was not properly presented until 24 March 1891 in the chapel of the Palace of Versailles by the Société l'Euterpe.[29] The strongest reception outside German-speaking countries was in England, true to its choral traditions. The work owed its support to a group centred on the Royal Academy of Music in London, which had close contacts with the composer's circle through Stockhausen, who, like Joachim and Clara Schumann, regularly performed in London. Stockhausen conducted the first, private, performance, as well as singing the baritone solos, at the residence of Sir Henry Thompson on 10 July 1871, with 'Fräulein Anna Regan' as soprano and 'a large number of ladies and gentlemen'; the accompaniments were played in piano duet form by Lady Thompson (the former musical prodigy Kate Loder) and the veteran Cipriani Potter. Next came a 'public rehearsal' of movements 1, 2, 5 and 6 under John Hullah, the conductor of the Academy orchestra. The work received its first full public performance on 2 April 1873 at St James's Hall at the Philharmonic Concert under W. G. Cusins with Sophie Ferrari and Charles Santley. George Macfarren, the Principal of the Royal Academy and Professor of Music at Cambridge, gave a warm review. 'It is impossible in the space of these comments even to hint at the extraordinary merit, technical and aesthetical, of the composition under our notice. When the German Requiem becomes known, lovers of music in England will feel indeed that their art has a living representative, that the greatest masters have a successor.'[30] But *The Musical Times*, like Hanslick, was much more noncommittal about the music, and more concerned with conventions of concert-giving:

Were we inclined to hazard an opinion upon the 'Requiem' from a single hearing, we certainly should not do so when performed as a concert piece, surrounded by composition in such violent contrast; and we must content ourselves therefore with saying that the un-emotional character of the subjects, notwithstanding the brilliancy of the instrumentation, produced a feeling of weariness in the audience, which, although we cannot accept as any tacit criticism of the work, sufficiently evidenced that the Philharmonic concert-room is not the place for a funeral service.[31]

The second English performance was again with the Philharmonic, on 6 April 1876.

The originality displayed in this 'Requiem' prevents anything like comparison with those masterpieces which have been bequeathed to us by the great composers who have passed away: it must be judged only as the earnest outpouring of an artist who feels the importance of his mission and dares to think for himself. Many of the movements are masterly specimens of constructive power; and the orchestral colouring, although in parts somewhat overladen, is generally in excellent tone with the subject of the text. The baritone solo, with chorus, 'Lord, make me to know the measure of my days' may be cited as one of the most impressive numbers of the work; and the choral pieces are written with due regard to the solemnity of the words, and a careful avoidance of mere display. The fault so observable in modern German music, of over-elaboration, is less apparent in this than in many other of the works of this composer.[32]

Thereafter the work was not performed again by the Philharmonic Society until the turn of the century. The primary performers became the newly formed Bach Choir, founded in 1875 as a specialist amateur choir to perform Bach and new choral music, of which the Brahms *Requiem* was the outstanding example. Unlike the Philharmonic, they were in a position to perform it to a general musical public rather than to members who were mainly performers. The Bach Choir, under Otto Goldschmidt, brought a much more dynamic approach to the work, preparing over a period of six months. The performance of 16 March 1880 was regarded as the 'best rendering of Brahms's German "Requiem" that has yet been given in this country . . . There may be reasons why a long time must pass before it can become generally popular, but musicians everywhere hold it in high honour.'[33] The singers were Mrs Osgood and George Henschel. But by the performance on 6 April of the following year, its problems were obviously receding for the choir, *The Musical Times* commenting that the Bach Choir 'was the first to give London amateurs a fair opportunity of hearing this work, and very little rehearsal could have been needed to secure even so fine a performance as that of which we now speak. The difficulties of the "Requiem" have been pointed out over and over again, together with the fact that, from their very nature, they must always remain difficulties, even in the experience of those who do no more than listen. But the music . . . steadily makes way amongst us, and we believe will win a permanent place.'[34] The difficulties were essentially in the vocal parts, unparalleled for performers of the time in their instrumental character in contrapuntal passages save in the works of Bach, which obviously explains the success of the choir in establishing the work. By May 1890 its establishment was complete, the Bach Choir ending its season – now under Charles Stanford's direction

– with 'abstract music not surpassed in beauty by any work of modern times'.[35] The first visiting German conductor to perform the *Requiem* in London appears to have been Hans Richter on 15 June 1891. In the second part of a programme of which the first was devoted to Wagner 'there was Brahms's noble German Requiem, which is rarely heard without gaining new friends'.[36] In the USA the work had first been heard in 1877, given by the New York Oratorio Society (of 400 singers) under Leopold Damrosch. It was generally well received with favourable comments on each movement, though not without reservation also. The first movement 'begins in an extremely simple, though noble and elevated style [and contains] . . . many beautiful passages which arise from . . . pleasing harmonic changes . . . [No 5] holds us spellbound with its charming development of the comforting theme, principally when it is taken up in an idealized and touching form by the tenors. The solo is beautifully interwoven and very effective . . . The last chorus . . . must be regarded as an anti-climax: still, the happy peaceful sentiment pervading its tone cannot be considered inconsistent with the state of mind inspired by the hearing of a work at once so elevating and sympathetic.'[37]

As in Germany, opposition in England was associated with the anti-academic figures, especially those devoted to Wagner, the most vociferous of whom was Bernard Shaw, who combined his reserve towards Brahms and towards English oratorio (at least as it was customarily performed) in a particular aversion to the *Requiem*. Though extreme, his view does reveal the features which alienated the Wagnerians while they pleased the Brahmsians. Every performance of the work by the Bach Choir or by Richter elicited a barbed review. Of the Bach Choir performance in 1890 Shaw comments on 'the intolerable tedium of sitting unoccupied whilst the Bachists conscientiously maundered through Brahms's Requiem. Mind, I do not deny that the Requiem is a solid piece of musical manufacture. You feel at once that it could only have come from the establishment of a first-class undertaker. But I object to requiems altogether.' He compares the work unfavourably with Mozart's Requiem, since 'there is no shadow of death anywhere in Mozart's music'.[38] On 24 June 1891 he writes in the *The World* of a performance by Richter. '[Brahms's] German Requiem was done from end to end, and done quite well enough to bring out all its qualities . . . the learned musicians [are delighted to explain] what a *point d'orgue* is [yet its elaborately modernized manner] makes the whole operation seem more desperately old fashioned and empty . . . Brahms seems to have been impressed by the fact that Beethoven created remarkable effects by persisting with pedal points long after Mozart would have resolved them . . . Only somehow it has not come off in Brahms's hands, though he has prolonged and persisted to the verge of human endurance.'[39] Although Shaw's expression of his views was humorously self-indulgent, it did anticipate the kinds of attitudes to major choral works, especially of the nineteenth century, which would emerge with the changing outlooks of the twentieth; though the greatest performers kept the *Requiem* alive as one of Brahms's supreme achievements.

5

The work in performance

Performance during Brahms's lifetime

Since Brahms conducted the first performance of the *German Requiem* himself and worked closely with Reinthaler in its preparation, a tradition of performance was established from the first. We can gain an idea of Brahms's intended tempi through the metronome marks for movements 1–4 and 6–7 appearing on the autograph full score and the copyist/part-autograph vocal score which were used in the rehearsals and Bremen performance.[1] During this period Brahms revised and refined the tempo characterizations, in some cases changing from Italian to German. Three sources partly chart the finalization of these markings from the completion of the full score until the preparation of the Bremen performance: the autograph full score; the copyist/part-autograph vocal score[2] and two vocal parts.[3] The full score bears the oldest markings in the case of movement 4 (where 'Andante' is deleted for the eventual 'Mäßig bewegt') and movement 7 (which is marked 'Andante con moto', a marking deleted for the eventual 'Feierlich' in the vocal score) and in the transition of movement 2, 'Aber des Herrn Wort . . .' (which appears as 'un poco animato', likewise a marking deleted in favour of the eventual 'un poco sostenuto' in the vocal score). Puzzling, however is the status of the two vocal parts, which ought to carry the later markings, but do not always do so: in movement 2a ('Denn alles Fleisch . . .') the marking is 'ziemlich langsam, marchmäßig' whilst the autograph full score and vocal score have the eventual 'langsam, marschmäßig'; movement 2 (tr) has 'un poco animato', like the original marking of the full score and vocal score; and, again, movement 7 has the original marking of the vocal score, 'Andante con moto', all suggesting an earlier stage of working and that Brahms was still holding different possibilities in mind in the three sources.[4] Comparison with the text sheet mentioned in Chapter 1 above (p. 11) shows how much of the work was once conceived at 'Andante' tempo.[5] The variants in the three sources are shown in Table 1, which also includes the markings of the first published edition.

Though these tempi established a framework for performance, the composer

Table 1. Brahms's expression and metronome markings in the autograph full score, copyist/part-autograph vocal score, vocal parts and first edition full score

Autograph full score	Copyist/part-autograph vocal score	Vocal parts	First edition
Movement 1			
a Ziemlich langsam und mit Ausdruck ♩= 80	SAME ♩= 80	SAME [No MM]	SAME ♩= 80
Movement 2			
a Langsam, marschmäßig ♩= 60	SAME ♩= 60	Ziemlich langsam, marschmäßig ♩= 60	Langsam, marschmäßig ♩= 60
b Etwas bewegter ♩= 80	SAME ♩= 80	SAME [No MM]	SAME ♩= 80
tr Un poco animato ♩= 56	poco (animato) sostenuto ♩= 56	Un poco animato [No MM]	poco sostenuto ♩= 56
c Allegro non troppo ♩= 108	SAME ♩= 108	SAME [No MM]	SAME ♩= 108
Movement 3			
a Andante moderato 𝅗𝅥= 52	SAME 𝅗𝅥= 52	SAME [No MM]	SAME 𝅗𝅥= 52
Movement 4			
1a (Andante) Mäßig bewegt ♩= 92	Mäßig bewegt ♩= 92	SAME [No MM]	SAME ♩= 92
Movement 5			
A Langsam ♪= 104	SAME ♪= [BLANK]		SAME ♪= 104
Movement 6			
a Andante ♩= 92	SAME ♩= 92	SAME [No MM]	SAME ♩= 92
b Vivace ♩= 112	[SAME] ♩= 112	SAME [No MM]	SAME ♩= 112
c Allegro 𝅗𝅥= 100	[SAME] 𝅗𝅥= 100	SAME [No MM]	SAME 𝅗𝅥= 100
Movement 7			
A Andante con moto ♩= 80	(Andante con moto) Feierlich ♩= 80	Andante con moto [No MM]	Feierlich ♩= 80

was never happy with the rigidity of metronome marks. He commented in later years 'I have never believed that my blood and a mechanical instrument go together' and that 'elastic' tempo was nothing new and should be taken 'con discrezione'.[6] In 1894 he asked his publisher to remove the marks from the published score. Having finally clarified his tempo and expression markings for the first edition, Brahms made no subsequent changes in later printings, which suggests that he was happy that tempi were not being unduly distorted in performance. His intentions would certainly have been known by conductors who gave early performances of the work, and the speeds noted by Blum from a private performance by Schubring differ only slightly from those of Brahms in being a little slower in the third and seventh movements.[7] Indeed, when another private performance of the work at Dessau in 1869 differed significantly, Max Bruch made a point of informing Brahms that the first movement had been 'almost adagio', the second movement 'rather too fast', the fourth 'andante cantabile, quasi adagio' and the sixth 'unbelievably lame'.[8] Though Brahms made no further amendments to the published score, some intended performance changes are revealed through the recollections of one performer who worked with him, Siegfried Ochs. Of the first vocal entry of movement 1 Ochs recalls 'Brahms wished to have the first three bars sung in the softest pianissimo, despite having written "p". He regarded it as an oversight that the choir was not indicated thus, as it is, where the orchestra enters at the third choral bar [b. 17].'[9] Brahms gave Ochs leave to vary the tempo for structural and expressive purposes in movement 4;[10] Ochs also notes that Brahms suggested the choir be in a tempo of quaver = 72 for the passage of repeated quavers at b. 21 and again at b. 24 of the fifth movement, 'thus very slow and to be sung with great expression'.[11] Since this is strikingly different from the marking given in 1868 for the movement it seems to show not merely that Brahms's idea of the tempo changed, but that he permitted great expression within passages as well as allowing for different performers and situations, a view confirmed in his comments elsewhere. The fact that an organ was not always available at the performance venue led Brahms to add a contrabassoon part,[12] though he seems to have preferred the use of the organ when available, as it was in the first Bremen performance. The exact size of the choir is not known, although, as Pascall notes, Brahms ordered 200 vocal parts and 12 each of the string parts for the Bremen performance.[13]

Performance in the twentieth century

By the end of Brahms's life in 1897, performance styles were changing with the rise of the 'interpretative conductor', responding to the increasing complexity of scores and size of orchestras, partly stimulated by the works of Wagner. Even conductors of the symphonic repertory that Brahms knew and admired were part of this tendency towards freer interpretation, not least of his own symphonies, for example Nikisch and Steinbach. Much as they were admired for their mastery, the fact that contemporary critics noted, for example, their variations in tempo from section to section, shows an awareness of radical changes in interpretation since Brahms's time. Markings for Brahms's *Requiem* recorded by Müller Reuter[14] show tempi becoming slower in the period 1890–1914, and the classical fast andante which still held good for Brahms, as for Bülow and others, yielding to its more leisurely modern meaning. For conductors born towards the end of Brahms's life and coming to full maturity between the wars, the performance assumptions had become very different, and tempo relationships had clearly changed in the Brahms *Requiem*. Three German conductors in the central tradition which linked to Brahms who made the work their own span the range of possibilities in the period: Bruno Walter (1876–1962), Otto Klemperer (1885–1973), Wilhelm Furtwängler (1886–1954). Each had his distinctive approach towards the musical structure and expression. They may be compared in recordings all made near the end of their lives: Furtwängler in 1948, Klemperer in 1962, Walter in 1954, first from the central standpoint of tempo and then from that of structure. Furtwängler was the most radical in his tempo range and expressive approach, and may be taken as the point of departure for a survey of some of the basic performance issues. Table 2 (p. 76) uses the formal designations of Chapter 3.

Furtwängler may be regarded as representing the most outstanding example of an 'interpretative' approach. His tempi show how slow the possible conception of a basic tempo had now become. They are the slowest by far in the performances considered here, though, partly for this reason, the subsections of movements show the greatest deviation from this basic tempo. The speed of only one movement relates to those indicated by Brahms, that of movement 4, though exactly so (crotchet = 92). The tempi of three of the movements are half the speed indicated by Brahms: thus, the overall tempo relationships are completely different. However, these relationships are clearly part of a plan in presenting the structure of the work, in which movements 1 and 7, 2 and 3, and 3 and 6 are carefully related, with movements 4 and 5 as a central contrast. Furtwängler's tempi for movements 1 and 7 allow for the reprise of movement 1 in movement 7 to come at its original tempo as a dramatic slowing at the point of thematic recall. The closely paired tempi for the outer sections of movements 2 and 3 give these movements a continuity which

Table 2. *Tempo relationships in the individual movements.*[15] *Furtwängler, Klemperer, Walter*

Furtwängler

Movement 1	Movement 2	Movement 3	Movement 4	Movement 5	Movement 6	Movement 7
a 44 (48 in recap)	a 44 (46)	a 46	1a 92	A 40	a 66	a 52
b 54–66	b 90	b 66–70		B 88	b 138	b 72
	c 118	c 116			c 120	1: a2 54

Klemperer

Movement 1	Movement 2	Movement 3	Movement 4	Movement 5	Movement 6	Movement 7
a 70	a 59	a 58	1a 100	A (54)	a 50	a 66
b 80	b 100	b 63		B (54)	b 120	b (72)
	c 120	c 69			c 110	1: a2 66

Walter

Movement 1	Movement 2	Movement 3	Movement 4	Movement 5	Movement 6	Movement 7
a 63–70	a 63	a 58	1a 100	A 54	a 88	a 69
b 80	b 120	b 63		B 60	b 150–60	b 72
	c 126	c 59			c 132	1: a2 69

enhances the effect of movement 3 as providing the climax of the first main structural division of the work. The tempi for movements 3 and 6 are quicker and balance each other. Thus the work is presented in a large three-part structure as 1–3; 4–6; 7 [1]. Many other means are used to articulate the larger structure. Focus on the conclusions of movements 3 and 6 is achieved by massive final fermatas, especially that in No. 3, which very clearly demarcates a structural division, and a slightly shorter one in movement 6 underpins the role of the fugue as a long dominant preparation for the concluding tonic. Flexibility of tempo within the movements themselves also effects the articulation of both the whole work and the individual movements. After the recall of the material of movement 1 in movement 7, the music gradually slows to a conclusion which matches the tentative opening of the work, and thus intensifies the relationship between the deep earthbound strings of the opening and the celestial woodwind chord at the end. The structural function of the coda is always emphasized in the performance; notably that of the fugue of movement 2, over a reflective pedal, and that of the sonata movement of movement 4, with its reflective recall of the opening idea. This approach is made more effective by the fact that some of the recapitulations are quicker than the expositions, as in movements 1 and 2. Most movements end with a slowing towards the final cadence, though the process is not automatic. Thus, though the fermata at the end of the pedal fugue of movement 3 is an inexorable consequence of the ritardando of the music which precedes it, the fugue of movement 6 ends more or less in tempo, the cumulative effect having been achieved through the great dynamic contrast of the distinctive homophonic passages in the latter part of the movement. In Furtwängler's treatment of tempi generally there is a suppleness which complements these larger-scale structural features and gives the sense of a living organism, an effect heightened by his use of dynamics: the remarkable hushed opening may have come directly to Furtwängler through Berlin tradition, of which both Ochs and later Furtwängler were a part.

The approach of Klemperer may be seen as representing an opposite view. If Furtwängler is regarded as romantic, Klemperer could be seen as classical, placing great emphasis on steady and unhurried tempi which are remarkably strict within the sections. Klemperer's tempo for movement 1 is much quicker than Furtwängler's, approaching that of Brahms at crotchet = 70. Movements 1 and 7 are at roughly the same tempo. Movement 2 is almost exactly at Brahms's marking, and like Furtwängler, he takes movements 1 and 2 as a pair. Klemperer is faster than both in movement 4, but very much more constrained in movement 6 at crotchet = 50, though the fugue increases to crotchet = 110, the mean of Furtwängler and Brahms. Within this large scheme, reflecting the relationships of 1 and 7, Klemperer is more interested in articulating the forms of the individual movements than in relating them. He is primarily concerned with orchestral balance and in revealing the contrapuntal texture, as at the opening where the imitative voices are plainly rather than tentatively presented. In movement 2 the horn chording of the funeral march stands out against the strict tempo with particular effect. He has been aptly described as a teutonic Michelangelo, shaping the score with sculptor's tools.[16]

Walter's tempi are less distinctive than those of these conductors. His tempo for No. 1 is much slower than that of Klemperer, though not as slow as that of Furtwängler. Again, there is a relationship between movements 1 and 7. His tempi for movements 3, 4 and 5 parallel Klemperer's. However, movement 6 is very different. He is the only one of the conductors so far discussed who begins this movement close to Brahms's marking. Moreover, he is quick through the entire movement, with a hectic march and impetuous fugue which has the structural effect of compressing the movement into a dramatic upbeat to No. 7 rather than a large preparation for it. This quality of spontaneity distinguishes his performance. If Furtwängler is reflective and Klemperer detached, Walter is warm and more immediately involved in the moment. He tends to accelerate within phrases, to make the music bloom through dynamic shaping, as at the choral opening, and this sense also comes through in his signalling of structural returns through the broadening of preceding cadences, as in movement 4. Dynamic changes for recapitulations are also notable, as in the cresendo in the da capo of the funeral march of the second movement.

These conductors set new standards for their successors, the generation born after Brahms's death and coming to full maturity after the Second World War. They might be compared in the recordings of three German conductors (see Table 3, p. 79) who widely performed Brahms, Herbert von Karajan (1908–91), Rudolf Kempe (1910–76) and Wolfgang Sawallisch (b. 1923). Karajan's recording is from 1956, Kempe's from 1955 and Sawallisch's from 1962.[17] Karajan is Furtwängler's most obvious musical successor. He follows Furtwängler's approach more closely than that of any others, though he does not take the outer movements as slowly and is slightly quicker in movement 2. But his tempi for the middle movements 3–6 are similar. There is evidence here of a comparable structural view, with Nos. 1–7 related exactly, and No 2 closely to No. 1. However, Karajan does not display the same degree of inner contrast, with a much narrower band of tempo changes, even where his basic tempo is the same. The similarity of tempo approach is mirrored in the expressive approach. Like Furtwängler, Karajan achieves a very hushed opening and

Table 3. *Tempo relations in individual movements: Karajan, Kempe, Sawallisch*

Karajan

Movement 1	Movement 2	Movement 3	Movement 4	Movement 5	Movement 6	Movement 7
a 54	a 58	a 46	1a 95	A 46	a 69	a 54
b 60	b 98	b 60		B 46	b 120	b 63
	c 112	c 108			c 108	1: a2 63

Kempe

Movement 1	Movement 2	Movement 3	Movement 4	Movement 5	Movement 6	Movement 7
a 56	a 56	a 52	1a 108	A 50	a 84	a 56
b (66)	b 112	b 60		B 54	b 144	b 62
	c 116	c 120			c 120	1: a2 51

Sawallisch

Movement 1	Movement 2	Movement 3	Movement 4	Movement 5	Movement 6	Movement 7
a 58	a 68	a 63	1a 116	A 52	a 112	a 64
b 66	b 108	b 69		B 60	b 144	b 69
	c 116	c 120			c 116	1: a2 63

a balancing conclusion to the work. But his desire above all for precision and polish of execution means that many passages appear deliberate, so that, though following the outline of Furtwängler's interpretation, he does not follow it in spirit. This is very clear in the rigid treatment of the transition bars of movement 2 'Aber des Herrn Wort', in the steady articulation of the pedal fugue of movement 3, and in the march and fugue of movement 6, where he makes an exact rhythmic relationship between the sections (two crotchets in 3/4 = one minim in 4/2). One very positive feature of his performance is the extent to which he reveals the orchestral fabric, often holding the choir back in a beautifully controlled legato while the orchestral detail is given prominence, pre-eminently in movement 4, revealing its purely instrumental character more than any of the conductors discussed.

Kempe follows Furtwängler's tempi in movement 3 (b, c) and 6 (b, c), but his other tempi are all quicker. In relative terms he unites movements 1 and 2 and makes a feature of a slower conclusion to the last movement. In expressive terms he tends towards the tempo fluctuation of Furtwängler and Karajan, but he is also capable of precision, especially at the transition in movement 2 and the following fugue, where he points the distinctive choral syncopations at 'wird weg müssen' and the contrast with 'seufzen' very carefully without losing the basic tempo. Sawallisch adopts a much quicker tempo throughout, though remaining relatively slow in the first movement, so that the performance displays a sense of growth and cumulation towards the end.

Current performance trends

The fact that such different types of performance can be effective reminds the listener of the two sides of Brahms's music so often noted by critics: the romantic and the classical. On the one hand, the richness of the musical language and its formal complexity encourages an approach which seeks to explore a deeper structural unity in the whole, as notably with Furtwängler, while, on the other, the numerous backward-looking features encourage a 'neo-classical' approach, where the emphasis lies rather on clarity and balance of sound, the score being read essentially as it stands. The latter type has become an issue in the modern performance of Brahms, since his music is now seen in a very different light. Though once considered a sign of conservatism, Brahms's rediscovery of the musical techniques of earlier periods and their synthesis in his own has come to be regarded as progressive by the culture of the present day. There is a certain aptness in the fact that it should be historically informed performers who are helping to project the rediscovery of the historical sources of the Brahms style, as the music of the Romantics comes into the purview of 'early music'. Two leading representatives of this trend have recently recorded the *Requiem*, John Eliot Gardiner and Roger Norrington.[18]

Both Gardiner and Norrington base their approach on instruments of the period and known performance practice. Roger Norrington writes at great length on his approach to Brahms.[19] Discussing the changes in orchestral instruments since c. 1870, he notes that the string instruments were not so different from those of the present, but that they used gut and gut-wound strings; the woodwind were improved from the classical form, but not as complex as today; the timpani were of leather, not plastic as today, with different sticks; the trombones were of narrower bore and the horns were hand-horns. The sound Brahms experienced would thus have been very different. In approaching string playing technique he takes the very few recordings of the time and Joachim's *Violin School* of 1904 as guides,[20] noting especially that there would have been little vibrato. The pitch would have been lower than today – about A = 435. As regards performance, Norrington recalls what is known of Brahms's tempo indications and of the size of orchestras of the time. Gardiner's discussion of the work is less detailed in historical performance background and more immediately concerned with the historical texture of the music. Gardiner observes that 'Brahms's most imposing choral work is often prey to performance of the solemn, unvaryingly smooth approach. The inherent rhythmic vitality and characteristic ruggedness of the masterpiece is often overlaid by a prevailing dinginess of texture and mood by what may be called "Wagnerian sostenuto" which is totally at variance with Brahms's own orchestral style.'[21] He aims to reinstate an 1860 orchestra, in order to expose the strata of Brahms's part-writing and the salient features of the choral and orchestral style, especially its polyphonic aspect. He cites the Viennese trombone in G, with its 'burnished mellow sound', the shorter Viennese oboe with its characteristic timbre, and the smaller brigher-sounding kettledrums with hard sticks. He says nothing on layout or size of the orchestra. As regards performance styles he echoes Norrington in his view of string technique, with the bow used as a means of expression mainly through variations of bow speed and pressure, with sparing use of vibrato for special emphasis only. He makes no comment on tempo or pitch.

The resulting performances reflect these different emphases. Their common features are obviously those of sound, owing to the nature of the instruments and the resulting balance between the instrumental sections. In both cases the wind, brass and timpani come through much more clearly in relation to the strings because of the smaller string sections and the lack of projecting vibrato. In general all the parts of the counterpoint can be heard, vocal and instrumental. The sound of the brass is perhaps the most distinctive feature, either in the full orchestral texture, where it contributes clarity to the bass line and – in the funeral march of the second movement – gives the harmony a special flavour or as an ensemble, particularly in the trombone passage from movement 7, 'Ja der Geist spricht, daß sie ruhen von ihrer Arbeit'. The string sound at the very opening of the work is also very striking, giving almost the effect of a viol consort of the seventeenth century. The flexibility arising from a smaller ensemble enables greater dynamic contrast within phrases, not least in the choir; both conductors use hairpin dynamics more than any of their predecessors except Walter. Norrington introduces some additional dynamics within choral lines, as in the fugue of No. 3, where they emphasize the harmonic movement. The performances differ most in the areas which are not mentioned by Gardiner in his discussion, articulation and tempi. Norrington places more emphasis on precise dynamic changes and a baroque-influenced approach to articulation and phrasing, seeking to complement the clarity of the orchestral sound. By comparison, Gardiner retains a more conventional performance style in bowing and dynamics. Norrington's dynamic range is not as great as Gardiner's; his smaller vocal forces give almost the effect of a chamber choir at the opening. On the other hand, Gardiner seems to be more concerned to make structural emphases, as, for example, in dramatic pauses at the repeated chords which precede the final dominant chord of the 'Vivace' of No. 6. The respective tempi are shown in Table 4.

Though they vary significantly in character, both these outstanding performances throw entirely new light on the work, whether in revealing details of the texture hitherto obscured or in the purity and virtuosity of the choral delivery. But they do not negate earlier achievements: nor can they be regarded as somehow definitive, when important questions remain unanswered. We do not know what size of performing forces Brahms preferred; the available range was very wide in his own day. And although we have evidence that slow to moderate tempi were taken faster in his time, we can never recapture the crucial flexibility which he seems to have taken for granted in other works, and which emerge from early recordings just after his lifetime. It is likely that the subtleties of this performing tradition (along with details of bowing and portamento) have gone for ever. Furtwängler's treatment of tempi is certainly subtle, but his particular flexibility has its roots in the performance of Wagnerian music drama rather than in the classical symphonic tradition; Brahms

Table 4. *Tempo relations in individual movements: Norrington and Gardiner*

Norrington

Movement 1	Movement 2	Movement 3	Movement 4	Movement 5	Movement 6	Movement 7
a 80	a 66	a 58	1a 104	A 56	a 100	a 90
b 86	b 116	b 80		B 63	b 142	b 72
		c 80			c 140	1:a2 75

Gardiner

Movement 1	Movement 2	Movement 3	Movement 4	Movement 5	Movement 6	Movement 7
a 66	a 63	a 63	1a 100	A 52	a 100	a 84
b 84	b 108	b 76		B 54	b 138	b 76
		c 64			c 106	1: a2 69

might have appreciated his grasp of large-scale structure, but he could hardly have condoned the individual tempi. The Brahms *Requiem* is now performed more frequently than ever before and there are many current recordings. But the problems which were stressed so strongly by the early critics still remain, despite modern performance standards. The realization of its many structural and expressive richnesses, whether in a concert-hall or church performance or in a recording, continues to pose a challenge.

Notes

1 Introduction

1 Letter of 9 October 1867. *Johannes Brahms im Briefwechsel* (hereafter *Brahms Briefwechsel*), vol. III (Berlin 1908), p. 10.

2 Hereafter, 'first performance' refers to the Bremen performance of the six movements without movement 5 on 10 April 1868 under Brahms; 'first complete performance' refers to the performance of the seven-movement work at Leipzig on 18 February 1869 under Karl Reinecke.

3 Carl Martin Reinthaler 1822–96: trained in theology as well as music; a pupil of A. B. Marx; organist of Bremen Cathedral from 1858 and conductor of the Bremen Singakademie 1858–90.

4 *Brahms Briefwechsel* III, p. 7.

5 Ibid., p. 10.

6 See Max Kalbeck, *Johannes Brahms*, 4 vols. (Berlin 1908–15), vol. II, pp. 235–6, note; see also Chapter 1 above, p. 8.

7 Brahms was prepared for his confirmation in 1848 by Pastor Johannes Geffcken, described by Niemann as a distinguished hymnologist and hymnbook editor. See Walter Niemann, *Johannes Brahms* (Berlin 1920); trans. C. A. Phillips as *Brahms* (New York 1929), p. 11.

8 *Brahms Briefwechsel* I, p. 200.

9 Letter of 21 July 1896 to Heinrich von Herzogenberg, *Brahms Briefwechsel* II, p. 75.

10 Brahms claimed in later years, 'In my study I can lay my hands on my Bible even in the dark'; quoted by Rudolf von der Leyen, *Johannes Brahms als Mensch und Freund* (Düsseldorf and Leipzig 1905), p. 32.

11 See Chapter 2 above for full discussion of the text.

12 1 Corinthians 13, verses 1–3, 12–23. I retain the traditional translation (also retained in the New English Bible) of the Latin 'caritas' for 'love' rather than 'charity', the most frequent alternative, in view of its more comprehensive meaning.

13 Brahms's comment was in response to Kalbeck's feuilleton 'Ein deutsches Requiem', first published by Kalbeck in *Die Presse*, 21 December 1888. See also Kalbeck, *Johannes Brahms*, vol. II, pp. 249–50.

14 As, for example, by Geiringer. See Karl Geiringer, *Brahms: His Life and Work*, 2nd edn, revised and enlarged with a new appendix of Brahms's letters (London 1963), p. 311.

15 The *Deutsches Requiem* (for SATB and organ) was written in 1818 to assist Ferdinand Schubert to obtain a post, and was until 1880 regarded as his own composition. It has five short sections. The German text is unconnected with that of Brahms's *Requiem*.

16 For discussion of the various forms of the Latin Requiem Mass see Christoph Wolff, *Mozart's Requiem: Historical and Analytical Studies, Documents, Sources*, trans. M. Whittall (Oxford 1994) pp. 65–71.

17 Berthold Litzmann, ed., *Clara Schumann–Johannes Brahms. Briefe aus den Jahren 1853–1896* (hereafter *Schumann–Brahms Briefe*), 2 vols. (Leipzig 1927; repr. Hildesheim and New York 1989), vol. I, p. 504. Brahms quotes the original text of the second movement here ('Denn alles Fleisch ist wie Gras', not his published version '. . . es ist wie Gras'); see below, Chapter 2, note 1.

18 *Schumann–Brahms Briefe*, p. 504.

19 Ibid., p. 508.

20 This is the view taken in the discussion of the background to the *Requiem* in the thematic catalogue of Brahms's works. (Margit L. McCorkle, *Johannes Brahms. Thematisch-bibliographisches Werkverzeichnis* (Munich 1984).) That the published correspondence was likely to contain such an error is, however, challenged by the fact that Brahms's friend Adolf Schubring made a similar mistake even later in reviewing the movement from the published score in the *Allgemeine musikalische Zeitung*, 4/2 (13 January 1869), p. 10, which is in B♭ minor (Schubring's review is discussed in Chapter 4, p. 64 and the manuscript/copyist material in Chapter 5, p. 72). Since he had no reason whatever to make such a mistake from the music before him he must have known either of Brahms's comment to Clara (perhaps through her) or of an earlier version of the music in C minor. If this version existed, it must have been a reworking/transposition of the original sonata/symphony, since C minor could not have been the key of an inner movement of a work in D minor. If it was, however, a slip on Brahms's part, it might have a subconscious relation to possible earlier influences upon this movement, for example Bach's chorale movement 'Wer weiß, wie nahe mir mein Ende', which is in C minor. See above, Chapter 2, p. 3.

21 *Schumann–Brahms Briefe*, vol. II, p. 504.

22 The autograph score resides in the Archive of the Gesellschaft der Musikfreunde, Vienna, to which it was donated by Brahms in 1893. It is described by Kalbeck (*Johannes Brahms*, vol. I, pp. 251–5) and Eusebius Mandyczewski (preface to the full score in vol. XVII of the *Sämtliche Werke*).

23 Albert Hermann Dietrich 1829–1908: composer and conductor; member of the Schumann circle from 1851; director of Music at Oldenburg from 1861 to 1890; lifelong friend of Brahms and performer of his works.

24 For the relationship of the two vocal scores of the *Requiem*, see above, Chapter 5 pp. 72–3.

25 *Bremer Courier*, 7 April 1868: 'we hear that it was completed in an intensive summer of 1866 and owes its inspiration to an earlier source . . . This is recalled in the outer form of the funeral march to the words "Denn alles Fleisch ist wie Gras und wie die Blume des Feldes" [sic].' ('Im äußeren form erinnert daran der Trauermarsch zu den Worten "Denn alles Fleisch . . ."')

26 Albert Dietrich, *Erinnerungen an Johannes Brahms* (Leipzig 1898), p. 45.

27 The evolution can be traced in Brahms's correspondence with Joseph Joachim and Clara Schumann and is summarized in McCorkle, *Werkverzeichnis*, pp. 170–1.

28 See Kalbeck, *Johannes Brahms*, vol. II, p. 250; Dietrich provided the information in response to Kalbeck's questionnaire 'Fragebogen für Herrn Hofkapellmeister Albert Dietrich (von Max Kalbeck)', in *Katalog – 100 Johannes Brahms: Musikantiquariat Hans Schneider* (Tutzing 1964), p. 12.

29 Kalbeck, *Johannes Brahms*, vol. II, p. 258.

30 Ibid, p. 50. See also S. Kross, *Die Chorwerke von Johannes Brahms* (Berlin and Wunsiedel 1958), pp. 219–22; and note 42 below.

31 Dietrich, *Erinnerungen an Brahms*, p. 58.

32 Ibid., p. 50.

33 Florence May, *The Life of Brahms*, 2 vols., 2nd revised edn (London 1948), vol. I, p. 388.

34 Dietrich, *Erinneringen an Brahms*, p. 61.

35 Brahms's first letter to Reinthaler, on 2 October 1867, was occasioned by the fact that he now knew the work to be in Reinthaler's possession. The correspondence continues with Reinthaler's reply of 5 October and Brahms's letter of 9 October quoted at the beginning of this chapter. See *Brahms Briefwechsel* III, pp. 5ff.

36 Richard von Perger, *Geschichte der k. k. Gesellschaft der Musikfreunde in Wien. I. Abteilung 1812 bis 1870* (Vienna 1912), p. 98.

37 See Kalbeck, *Johannes Brahms*, vol. II, p. 262.

38 The D pedal which concludes the movement had caused major performance difficulties in Vienna. Brahms wrote to Marxsen (apparently thereafter in December 1867), commenting of the 'eternal D' that 'if I do not use the organ, it does not sound'. Quoted in Kalbeck, *Johannes Brahms*, vol. II, p. 232. See further on the status of the organ (ad lib.) part and its relation to the contrabassoon part, below, p. 89, note 3.

39 Berthold Litzmann, *Clara Schumann. Ein Künstlerleben nach Tagebüchern und Briefen*, 3 vols. (Leipzig 1902–8), vol. III, pp. 218–19.

40 *Brahms Briefwechsel* XIV (Berlin 1920), p. 152.

41 May quotes the comment in her *Life of Brahms*, vol. II, p. 415. Deiters was Brahms's first signif- icant biographer; his *Johannes Brahms*, appeared in the series *Sammlung musikalischer Vorträge* (2nd series, 23/24 (1880)) and was followed by *Johannes Brahms* (Leipzig 1898).

42 Movements 1 and 2 were marked 'Andante'. Kalbeck's interpretation (see above, note 30) of the sheet to show movements 1–4 as a group is based on the differences in ink used as between movements 1–4 and 5–7, dating the former with the draft for No. 4 of the *Magelonelieder* on the recto of the sheet. See above, Chapter 5, p. 72–4 for the final revisions to the tempo markings and the relation of the sheet to them.

43 A. Steiner, *Johannes Brahms, I. Teil. 86 Neujahrsblatt der Allgemeine Musikgesellschaft in Zürich* (Zurich 1898), p. 21.

44 For discussion of the text of movement 5, see above, Chapter 2, pp. 20, 22; for the music, Chapter 3, pp. 47–50.

45 'der hoffentlich erst recht ein Ganzes aus dem Werk macht'. *Brahms Briefwechsel* XIV, p. 153.

46 May, *Life of Brahms*, vol. II, p. 412, note.

47 Ibid., p. 374.

48 *Brahms Briefwechsel* VI, p. 88. Parallels between the *Requiem* and Schumann choral works have been made by Blum (with *Requiem für Mignon*) in *Hundert Jahre Ein deutsches Requiem*, pp. 101–7 and Christopher Reynolds (with *Das Paradies und die Peri*) in 'A Choral Symphony by Brahms?', *Nineteenth-Century Music*, 9/1 (1985), pp. 3–25. I owe to Professor Brian Trowell the observation of the parallel between the harmonic progression and part movement of bb. 1–4 of movement 1 of the *Requiem* and bb. 1–2 of the first movement of Schumann's Piano Quintet, and of links between the following section a2 of the Brahms and the finale of the Schumann work (Brahms bb. 29ff, Schumann bb. 94ff).

49 See May, *Life of Brahms*, vol. II, p. 433.

50 Mandyczewski cites Brahms's growing reserve about the unison scoring of voices in the final section of movement 4, bb. 154–64. See Chapter 5, p. 000 for other examples of his later inten- tions for revision. He also quotes passages revised between the autograph full score and the first edition. Sketches exist of parts of movements 6 and 7 only. They throw no light on the origins of the work, though they show interesting aspects of the progress of Brahms's thought at an early stage of drafting the continuity of certain passages. See McCorkle, *Werkverzeichnis*, p. 174. No. 6 is discussed in Paul Mies, 'Aus Brahms' Werkstatt', *Simrock Jahrbuch* I (Berlin 1928), p. 42.

2 The work as a whole

1 However, in movement 6, Brahms retains an original spelling in 'Denn wir haben *hie* . . .' The most notable emendations are in the following passages, of which the original texts are: in move- ment 2, 'Denn alles Fleisch ist wie Gras'; in movement 3, 'Aber, Herr, lehre doch mich', 'Wie gar nichts sind alle Menschen' and 'Aber, der Gerechten Seelen'; in movement 5, 'Und ihr habt auch nun Traurigkeit'; in movement 6, 'zur Zeit der letzten Posaune'. Additionally, he changes the phrase in movement 6 'Denn du hast alle Dinge geschaffen' to 'erschaffen' at the final state- ment from bar 290.

2 Author's translation. The numbering of the verses follows that in the Authorized Version and *The New English Bible*, which differs in some cases from that of the Luther Bible.

3 The translation of this passage shows a great difference between the Luther Bible and the English versions. *The New English Bible* includes the name Christ and has different syntax. The entire verse reads as follows: 'Moreover, I heard a voice from heaven, saying "Write this: 'Happy are the dead who die in the faith of Christ! Henceforth', says the Spirit, 'they may rest from their labours, for they take with them the record of their deeds.'"'

4 See above, Chapter 1, note 1.

5 Franz Grasberger, *Johannes Brahms 'Ihr habt nun Traurigkeit', 5. Satz aus dem 'Deutschen Requiem'. Faksimile der ersten Niederschrift* (Tutzing 1968), p. 9. The facsimile edition, which

includes Grasberger's remarks as part of the introduction, is taken from the vocal score given by Brahms to Clara Schumann at Christmas 1866. See also below, Chapter 5, note 2. The motive has been identified by several writers, and the examples given merely indicate the most obvious uses of the motive, some writers drawing myriad shapes from the work by quasi-serial procedures of retrograde and inverted retrograde relationship. See the presentations of John Gardner, 'A Note on Brahms's "Requiem", *The Musical Times*, 95 (1964), p. 649; William S. Newman, 'A "Basic Motive" in Brahms's "German Requiem"', *Music Review*, 24 (1963), p. 190; Hans Hollander, 'Gedanken zum strukturellen Aufbau des Brahmsschen "Requiems"', *Schweizerische Musikzeitung*, 105/6 (1965), pp. 326–33; Malcolm Boyd, 'Brahms's Requiem: A Note on Thematic Integration', *The Musical Times*, 113 (1972), pp. 140–1.

6 Siegfried Ochs, preface to Eulenburg Edition, No. 969, p. iv. Text and melody of the chorale are by Georg Neumark (1621–81) and first appeared in his *Fortgepflantzter Musikalisch-Poetischer Lustwald* (Jena, 1657).

7 Siegfried Ochs, *Geschehenes, Gesehenes* (Leipzig 1922) p. 302; Siegfried Ochs, *Das deutsche Gesangverein für gemischten Chor*, 3 vols. (Berlin 1926), vol. III, p. 159.

8 See Johannes Zahn, *Die Melodien der deutschen evangelischen Kirchenlieder*, 3 vols. (Gütersloh 1890, repr. Hildesheim 1963), vol II, No. 2778, note.

9 See Michael Musgrave, 'Historical Influences on Brahms's "Requiem"', *Music and Letters*, 53/1 (January 1972), pp. 3–17 and Reynolds, 'A Choral Symphony by Brahms?', pp. 3–25. Though the thematic parallel between 'Freu' dich sehr, O meine Seele' is strong in the opening bars of movement 1, parallels between this phrase and other parts of the *Requiem* are by no means as striking or generative in the case of the chorale Ochs specifies (see above, pp. 26–9). Nor does the text of this chorale have the same emphasis on sorrow and misfortune transformed by hope, which is such a link between the other cantata texts and the Schumann song cited on p. 33 above and 'Wer nur . . .': its tone is much more optimistic, consistent with its major-mode melody. Moreover, its specific reference to Christ ('Christ the Lord for you is calling') as well as to *Elijah* seems to fit ill with Brahms's obvious avoidance of the name in the *Requiem*. Finally, the fact that Brahms asked a seemingly joking question of Schubring as to whether he had uncovered the 'political reference' for the year 1866 in his *Requiem* – alluding to the similarity between the work's opening notes and the melody 'Gott erhalte . . .' (the Austrian imperial hymn) – seems to discourage too much emphasis on this theme, the opening notes of which are, like those of 'Wer nur', commonplace (letter of 16 February 1869, *Brahms Briefwechsel* VIII, p. 215, note 2).

10 Kalbeck, *Johannes Brahms*, vol. I, p. 276.

11 *Brahms Briefwechsel* IV, p. 9.

12 Noted by R. H. Schauffler, *The Unknown Brahms* (New York 1933), p. 33.

13 This translation of 'Wer nur den lieben Gott läßt walten' is by Catherine Winkworth and begins 'If thou but suffer God to guide thee / and hope in Him through all thy ways / He'll give thee strength whate'er betide thee / and bear thee through the evil days' (*The Chorale Book for England* (London 1863; 2nd enlarged edn 1864)).

14 For further discussion of this relationship see Musgrave, 'Historical Influences'.

15 The suggestion by A. Tilden Russell that Brahms 'composed the melody himself and only later recognized its coincidental similarity to one or more pre-existing melodies' assumes that he later overlooked such a relationship in stating to Ochs that the melody (or its source) *was* a chorale. See A. Tilden Russell, 'Brahms and *Wer nur den lieben Gott lässt walten:* A New Contribution', *Newsletter of the American Brahms Society*, 6/2 (Autumn 1988); see also above, Chapter 1, p. 6 and note 29.

16 See further Musgrave, 'Historical Influences'.

3 The individual movements

1 This results in either large-scale repetition in the musical form, or in subdivisions of the text into closed musical forms. Bach's B minor Mass, for example, sets its text in twenty-four movements, each as aria, duo, choral fugue, etc.

2 Brahms's song aesthetic is outlined by his pupil Gustav Jenner in *Johannes Brahms als Mensch, Lehrer und Künstler* (Marburg 1905), pp. 31 ff.

3 The indication 'for at least two harps' is included in the Collected Edition but not in the Eulenburg score. It is confirmed in Brahms's correspondence and in the advertisements for the first performance. The designation 'ad lib.' for the organ and contrabassoon parts seems to mean that Brahms wished the contra to play in the absence of the organ, but not when an organ was available. His comment to Marxsen (see above, p. 86, note 38) was occasioned by the fact that the venue of the Viennese part-performance on 1 December 1867, the Grosse Redoutensaal, had no organ. For a summary of the issues see also Robert Pascall, 'The Organ and Contrafagotto in Brahms's German Requiem', letter to the editor, *The Musical Times*, 133 (January 1992), p. 7.

4 As implied by A. F. Thibaut in *Über Reinheit der Tonkunst* (Heidelberg 1825); trans. J. Broadhouse as *Purity in Music* (London 1882), pp. 59–60. His earlier comment (p. 27) on the association of the common chord with the style of 'pure' vocal music in works by Lasso and Palestrina also bears on Brahms's style in this passage. See further my discussion on p. 42.

5 See Chapter 2, pp. 26ff for reference to the role of the chorale in the work.

6 Comparison with a more conventional harmonic setting of a similar melodic outline in a nineteenth-century work well known to Brahms makes this clear. 'Cast thy burden upon the Lord' from Mendelssohn's *Elijah* has a closely related syllabic structure, but results in more regular phrasing. Indeed, the parallel between these passages may well not be fortuitous. The full original title of 'Wer nur den lieben Gott läßt walten' includes the text: 'A Song of Comfort. God will care for and help every one in His own own time. Cast thy burden upon the Lord and he shall sustain thee' (Psalm 55, verse 22). See above, p. 88, note 6.

7 This passage is the first of several in the 'non-fugal movements' to illustrate the comment Brahms made of the quasi-fugal passage of movement 4 (bb. 125ff). Tovey notes (presumably from his direct contact with Joachim) that 'Once, when Joachim was deploring the growing tendency of composers to reduce choral writing to a lazy, degenerate mass of chords, doubled in octaves, Brahms said in reference to this passage [movement 4] "Ah, I set them a bad example there!"' See Donald Francis Tovey, *Essays in Musical Analysis*, 6 vols. (London 1935–9); vol. V, *Vocal Music* (London 1937), p. 220.

8 Tovey describes this movement as a 'Viennese ländler', giving no apparent acknowledgement of its chorale-like quality. See Tovey, *Essays*, vol. V, p. 214. It is sometimes referred to as a 'dance' of death because of its triple metre, though Brahms's comment to Clara and tempo characterizations refer to 'march'.

9 *Marienlieder* No. 5, 'Ruf zur Maria' (composed c. 1859, published 1862).

10 Notable examples are the codas of the variation movements of the String Sextets Opp. 18 and 36.

11 The text of Op. 32/1 includes the lines 'Ah, speak, say just one word, only reveal your true feelings to me'; that of Op. 32/2 includes the words 'You have squandered the day, you seek light in the night . . . for time runs on and does not return' (translations by Henry S. Drinker).

12 In the Serenade for Orchestra Op. 16 Brahms also omits violins and gives the woodwind a prominent part.

13 For some suggestions of links to the discarded symphony via the First Piano Concerto see Reynolds, 'A Choral Symphony by Brahms?', pp. 14–18.

14 The counter-subject was first scored for oboe and bassoon in Brahms's autograph and bassoon in the proof, but transferred to the oboe in the first edition proper.

15 The *Schicksalslied* was completed in 1871 and published in the same year.

16 Brahms's subject resembles that of the fugue which concludes Mendelssohn's Organ Sonata in C minor Op 37/2 particularly when a running counter-subject is added at b. 39 of the Mendelssohn. Moreover, the introduction to Brahms's fugue (with the subject emerging from a long-held final chord at the end of the preceding Vivace) may owe something to a similar device in movements 3 and 4 (un-numbered) of the Mendelssohn.

17 Symphony in E♭ major Op. 97; composed 1850, Düsseldorf. The movements of the Requiem Mass marked 'Feierlich' are No. 2 'Te decet hymnus' and No. 6 'Domine Jesu Christe'; in addition two movements following No. 6 are marked 'at the same tempo'. The marking of the third

movement 'Ziemlich bewegt' is, like that of the opening of the Fourth Symphony ('Ziemlich langsam'), characteristic of Schumann. It is therefore of interest that Brahms uses the term 'ziemlich langsam' both in the first movement and in an earlier marking of the second movement ('Ziemlich langsam und mit Ausdruck' and 'Ziemlich langsam, marschmäßig'). See Chapter 5, pp. 72–3.

18 J. S. Bach, *St Matthew Passion*, No. 29: 'O Mensch, bewein dein Sünde groß'. Brahms knew the work very well and later performed it with the Musikverein of the Gesellschaft der Musikfreunde during his directorship, in March 1875.

19 In 1863 Brahms directed the Vienna Singverein in one item from Schütz's *Symphoniae Sacrae III*, 'Saul, Saul, was verfolgst du mich?', taking his text from Carl von Winterfield, *Johannes Gabrieli und sein Zeitalter* (Berlin 1843).

4 Reception

1 Perger, *Geschichte der k. k. Gesellschaft der Musikfreunde in Wien, I. Abteilung*, p. 98.

2 *Die neue freie Presse*, Vienna, 3 December 1867. Also published in summarized form in *Allgemeine musikalische Zeitung*, 2/15 (1867), pp. 408–9.

3 Ibid.

4 Summarized and translated by May, *Life of Brahms*, vol. II, pp. 395–6.

5 Ibid., p. 395.

6 Letter of 1 December 1867. *Briefe von und an Joseph Joachim*, coll. and ed. Johannes Joachim and Andreas Moser, 3 vols. (Berlin 1911–13); trans. N. Bickley as *Letters to and from Joseph Joachim* (London 1914), p. 370.

7 Theodor Billroth, *Briefe von Theodor Billroth* (Hanover and Leipzig 1906), p. 88 (author's translation).

8 *Weser Zeitung*, 29 March 1868. Quoted in Blum. *Hundert Jahre Ein deutsches Requiem*, p. 44.

9 *Bremer Courier*, 10 April 1868. Quoted in Blum, *Hundert Jahre Ein Deutsches Requiem*, p. 60.

10 Ibid.

11 *Neue Zeitschrift für Musik*, 35 (10 April 1868), p. 35.

12 Angelika Horstmann, *Untersuchungen zur Brahms-Rezeption der Jahre, 1860–1880* (Hamburg 1986), p. 174.

13 Fritzsch's attitude to Brahms in reviews in the *Musikalisches Wochenblatt* is discussed by Siegfried Kross in 'The Establishment of a Brahms Repertoire', *Brahms 2: Biographical, Documentary and Analytical Studies*, ed. M. Musgrave (Cambridge 1985), pp. 21–38.

14 May, *Life of Brahms*, vol. II, p. 433.

15 Horstmann, *Untersuchungen*, pp. 174, 176.

16 Adolf Schubrings '"Schumanniana Nr. 12". Ein deutsches Requiem . . . von Johannes Brahms', *Allgemeine Musikalische Zeitung*, 4/2–3 (January 1869), pp. 9–11, 19–20.

17 Ibid. This analysis is extremely inadequate in that it identifies chords with keys, rather than interpreting the upper parts as elaborating the chord of F, the root of which is held throughout in the pedal.

18 Ibid.

19 Amadeus Macewski, 'Ein deutsches Requiem . . . von Johannes Brahms', in *Musikalisches Wochenblatt*, January 1870. Quoted and summarized by Horstmann in *Untersuchungen*, p. 150.

20 Horstmann, *Untersuchungen*, p. 149.

21 Richard Specht, *Johannes Brahms. Leben und Werk eines deutschen Meisters* (Hellerau 1928); trans. E. Blom as *Johannes Brahms* (London 1930), p. 206.

22 P. Kleinert, 'Ein deutsches Requiem', in *Neue evangelische Kirchenzeitung*, 13 March 1869. Quoted in Horstmann, *Untersuchungen*, p. 137.

23 Richard Wagner, *The Prose Works of Richard Wagner*, trans. W. A. Ellis, 8 vols. (London 1892–9); vol. VI, *Religion and Art*, p. 21.

24 Review by Franz Gehring for the *Allgemeine Musikzeitung*, quoted in May, *Life of Brahms*, vol. II, p. 461. This first complete performance on 5 June 1872 was Levi's farewell concert from the Grand Ducal Orchestra and Philharmonic Society.

25 Ochs, preface to Eulenburg Edition No. 969, p. iv.

26 Listed by Kalbeck, *Johannes Brahms*, vol. II, appendix II, pp. 281–3.

27 D'Indy took a copy of the work, inscribed by the composer, to Brahms, though it was received with indifference. See Vincent d'Indy, *César Franck*, trans. and with an introduction by Rosa Newmarch (London 1910; repr. New York 1965), p. 112.

28 Hugues Imbert, *Johannes Brahms* (Paris 1906), p. 153.

29 Hugues Imbert, 'Le Requiem de Brahms', *Portraits et Etudes* (Paris 1894), p. 125.

30 George Alexander Macfarren, Notes to the Programme of the Philharmonic Concert of 2 April 1873. The work was sung in English, the vocal score with English words having appeared in 1872 (Rieter-Biedermann, Leipzig and Winterthur).

31 *The Musical Times*, 16 (May 1873), p. 75.

32 *The Musical Times*, 17 (May 1876), p. 401.

33 *The Musical Times*, 21 (April 1880), p. 174.

34 *The Musical Times*, 22 (May 1881), p. 244.

35 *The Musical Times*, 31 (June 1890), p. 346.

36 *The Musical Times*, 32 (July 1891), p. 408.

37 *Dwight's Journal of Music*, 37/1 (17 April 1877), p. 4.

38 G. B. Shaw, ed. Dan H. Laurence, *Shaw's Music*, 3 vols. (London 1981), vol. II, p. 67.

39 Ibid., p. 376.

5 The work in performance

1 Though these are not in Brahms's hand, they clearly came from him or had his approval. He elaborates them in a letter to his publisher of 1 October 1868 (*Brahms Briefwechsel* XIV, p. 164), adding a marking for movement 2c (crotchet = 108) and the added, fifth, movement (quaver = 104).

2 There are two surviving part-autograph scores, one resident in the Brahms Institut, Lübeck, and one in the Hamburg Stadt- und Universitätsbibliothek. Both have Brahms's full autograph of the added fifth movement inserted into the original six-movement sequence. The Lübeck score is marked for the conductor and contains metronome marks; it also contains autograph revisions, some substantial, and was clearly used as the engraver's model for the first edition of the vocal score. The Hamburg score (which was that given to Clara Schumann: No. 5 is published in facsimile – see Chapter 2, note 5) appears to have been the model for the Lübeck score, and the first few pages have the piano part in Brahms's hand as a guide to the copyist; however, in the case of the fifth movement, Brahms seems to have copied from his autograph in the Lübeck score. Both scores are discussed by Friedrich G. Zeileis. 'Two Manuscript Sources of Brahms's German Requiem', *Music and Letters*, 60 (1979), pp. 149–55. The Lübeck score is further discussed by Michael Struck: 'Ein deutsches Requiem – handlich gemacht. Der Klavierauszug und seine Stichvorlage', *Patrimonia* 80 (Kulturstiftung der Länder; Kiel, 1994), pp. 5–18.

3 One soprano and one alto part in lithographic copy of the six-movement version of the *Requiem* reside in the Sammlung Hofmann, Lübeck, as materials from the Bremen performance. They differ not only from the published score in tempo characterizations, but also from the text-sheet of the entire work, showing its markings for movements 1 and 2 (Andante, Andante) to pre-date the final revisions in the preparations for the first performance. See also Chapter 1, p. 11 and note 42.

4 Even the proof copy of the first edition of the full score (numbered Op. 48) shows hesitation through the omission of some important markings, generally added in pencil by Brahms. I am indebted to the Director, Kurt Hofmann, for providing me with access to this and to the vocal score and parts noted above.

5 See chapter 1, p. 11 and note 42.

6 George Henschel, *Musings and Memories of a Musician* (London 1918), pp. 313–14.

7 Blum, *Hundert Jahre Ein deutsches Requiem*, p. 119.

8 *Brahms Briefwechsel* III, pp. 95–6.

9 Siegfried Ochs, *Das deutsche Gesangverein für gemischten Chor*, 3 vols. (Berlin 1923–6), vol. III, p. 159.

10 Ibid., p. 169.

11 Ibid., pp. 168–9.

12 See above, p. 89, note 3.

13 Robert Pascall, 'Historical Perspectives on Brahms's Ein deutsches Requiem', notes on the Norrington recording EMI CD CDC754658–2, p. 5. It is impossible to specify the numbers on the basis of the membership listing for the season 1867–8 alone. I am indebted to Dr Ann Kersting of the Bremen Staats- und Universitätsbibliothek for examining the *Protokollbuch* of the Singakademie and informing me that the choir had no more rehearsals for the work than for other performances, and that it was certainly augmented in size by singers from surrounding districts.

14 Theodor Müller Reuter, *Lexicon der deutschen Konzertliteratur* (Leipzig 1921), p. 172.

15 Furtwängler (Lindberg-Torlind, Sonnerstedt, Musikaliska Sallskapet Kor, Stockholms Konsertforenings Orkester) Music and Arts CD-298 (2); Walter (Seefried, London, Westminster Choir, New York Philharmonic) CBS CD CB 701; Klemperer (Schwarzkopf, Fischer Dieskau, Philharmonia Chorus, Philharmonia Orchestra) EMI CD C7 47238-2.

The metronome markings of this table and Tables 3 and 4 follow the tactus indications in Table 1, p. 73, except for movement 5, which is given in crotchets. The marking is of the basic tempo for the main idea of each section, usually the opening statement.

16 Roger Dettmer, Notes to the Furtwängler recording, p. 5.

17 Karajan (Janowitz, Waechter, Vienna Singverein, Vienna Symphony Orchestra) CD DG Galleria 427252-2; Kempe (Grümmer, Fischer-Dieskau, Choir of St Hedwig's Cathedral, Berlin Philharmonic) CD EMI Classics CDH 64705; Sawallisch (Lipp, Cranz, Vienna Symphony Orchestra, Singverein der Gesellschaft der Musikfreunde) CD Philips CD 438760-2.

18 Gardiner (Margiano, Gilfry, Monteverdi Choir, Orchestre Révolutionnaire et Romantique) P CD 432 140-4PH; Norrington (Dawson, Bär, Schütz Choir of London, London Classical Players) EMI CD CDC754658-2.

19 Norrington discusses the orchestral dimension of Brahms performance at greatest length in connection with the First Symphony: 'Aimez-vous Brahms?', *Gramophone* (October 1991), pp. 67–8. Performance aspects of his recording of the *Requiem* are discussed in Pascall 'Historical Perspectives on Brahms's Ein deutsches Requiem'.

20 Joseph Joachim with Andreas Moser, *Violinschule*, 3 vols. Berlin 1902–5; 2nd edn, ed. M. Jacobsen (1959).

21 John Eliot Gardiner, 'Brahms and the "Human" Requiem', *Gramophone* (April 1990), p. 1809.

Select bibliography

Beller-McKenna, Daniel, 'Brahms, the Bible and Robert Schuman', *Newsletter of the American Brahms Society*, 13/2 (Autumn 1995), pp. 1–4.

Billroth, Theodor, *Briefe von Theodor Billroth* (Hanover and Leipzig 1906).

Blum, Klaus, *Hundert Jahre Ein deutsches Requiem von Johannes Brahms* (Tutzing 1971).

Boyd, Malcolm, 'Brahms's Requiem: A Note on Thematic Integration', *The Musical Times*, 113 (1972), 140–1.

Brahms, Johannes, *Johannes Brahms. Briefwechsel*, 16 vols. (Berlin 1908–22, repr. Tutzing 1974). Vols I and II: *Johannes Brahms im Briefwechsel mit Heinrich u. Elisabet von Herzogenberg*, ed. M. Kalbeck, 1921. Vol. III: *Johannes Brahms im Briefwechsel mit Karl Reinthaler, Max Bruch, Hermann Deiters, Karl Reinecke, Ernst Rudorff, Bernhard und Luise Scholz*, ed. W. Altmann, 1908. Vol. IV: *Johannes Brahms im Briefwechsel mit J. O. Grimm*, ed. R. Barth, 1908. Vols V and VI: *Johannes Brahms im Briefwechsel mit Joseph Joachim*, ed. A. Moser, 1921, 1912. Vol. VIII: *Johannes Brahms im Briefwechsel mit J. V. Widmann, Ellen und Ferdinand Vetter und Adolf Schubring*, ed. M. Kalbeck, 1915. Vol. XII: *Johannes Brahms im Briefwechsel mit J. P. Simrock und Fritz Simrock*, ed. M. Kalbeck, 1919. Vol. XIV: *Johannes Brahms im Briefwechsel mit Breitkopf und Härtel, Bartholf Senff, J. Rieter-Biedermann, C. F. Peters, E. W. Fritszch und Robert Lienau*, ed. Wilhelm Altmann, 1920.

Ein deutsches Requiem nach Worten der heil. Schrift (Leipzig and Winterthur: J. Rieter-Biedermann, 1869).

Ein deutsches Requiem nach Worten der heil. Schrift, in *Brahms, Sämtliche Werke*. Ausgabe der Gesellschaft der Musikfreunde in Wien, ed. E. Mandyczewski and H. Gál, 27 vols. (Leipzig: Breitkopf und Härtel, 1926–8). Vol. XXVII; reprinted with English translation of the editorial commentary and text (New York: Dover Publications, 1987).

Ein deutsches Requiem op. 45, with Vorwort by Siegfried Ochs and Foreword by Anthony Bruno (London: Edition Eulenburg 969, n.d [c. 1900]).

Ein deutsches Requiem nach Worten der heil. Schrift [vocal score] (Leipzig and Winterthur: J. Rieter-Biedermann, 1869).

Requiem by Joh. Brahms, op. 45 [vocal score with English text] (Leipzig and Winterthur: J. Rieter-Biedermann, 1872).

J. Brahms, Requiem [vocal score], ed. John E. West, preface by Ernest Newman (London: Novello, 1910).

Biblia, das ist die ganze Heilige Schrift Deudsch (Wittenberg 1534) [The first edition of Luther's translation].

The Holy Bible (London 1611) [English Authorized Version, 'King James').

The New English Bible (Oxford and Cambridge 1970).

Deiters, Hermann, *Johannes Brahms, in Sammlung musikalischer Vorträge* 2nd series, 23/24 (1880).

Dietrich, Albert, *Erinnerungen an Johannes Brahms* (Leipzig 1898).

D'Indy, Vincent, *César Franck*, trans. and with an introduction by Rosa Newmarch (London 1910; repr. New York 1965).

Gál, Hans, *Johannes Brahms. Werk und Persönlichkeit* (Frankfurt 1961), trans. J. Stein, as *Brahms: His Work and Personality* (London 1963).

Gardiner, John Eliot, 'Brahms and the "Human" Requiem', *Gramophone* (April 1990), pp. 1809–10.

Gardner, John, 'A Note on Brahms's "Requiem"', *The Musical Times*, 95 (1964), p. 649.

Geiringer, Karl, *Brahms: His Life and Work*, 2nd edn, revised and enlarged with a new appendix of Brahms's letters (London 1963).

Grasberger, Franz, *Johannes Brahms 'Ihr habt nun Traurigkeit', 5. Satz aus dem 'Deutschen Requiem'. Faksimile der ersten Niederschrift* (Tutzing 1968).

Henschel, George, *Musings and Memories of a Musician* (London 1918).

Hofmann, Renate, 'Vier Briefe des Verlegers J. Rieter-Biedermann an Johannes Brahms', *Patrimonia*, 80 (1994), pp. 13–26.

Holländer, Hans, 'Gedanken zum strukturellen Aufbau des Brahmsschen "Requiem"', *Schweizerische Musikzeitung* 105/6 (1965), pp. 326–33.

Horstmann, Angelika, *Untersuchungen zur Brahms-Rezeption der Jahre 1860–1880* (Hamburg 1986).

Imbert, Hugues, 'Le Requiem de Brahms', *Portraits et Etudes* (Paris 1894).

Johannes Brahms (Paris 1906).

Jenner, Gustav, *Johannes Brahms als Mensch, Lehrer und Künstler* (Marburg 1905).

Joachim, Joseph, *Briefe von und an Joseph Joachim*, coll. and ed. Johannes Joachim and Andreas Moser, 3 vols. (Berlin 1911–13); trans. N. Bickley as *Letters to and from Joseph Joachim* (London 1914).

Joachim, Joseph, with Andreas Moser, *Violinschule*, 3 vols. (Berlin 1902–5); 2nd edn, ed. M. Jacobsen (1959).

Kalbeck, Max, 'Fragebogen für Herrn Hofkapellmeister Albert Dietrich (von Max Kalbeck), in *Katalog – 100 Johannes Brahms: Musikantiquariat Hans Schneider* (Tutzing 1964).

Johannes Brahms, 4 vols. (Berlin 1908–15).

'Ein deutsches Requiem von Johannes Brahms' (Feuilleton), *Die Presse*, 21 December 1888.

Kross, Siegfried, *Die Chorwerke von Johannes Brahms* (Berlin and Wunsiedel 1958).

Litzmann, Berthold, *Clara Schumann. Ein Künstlerleben nach Tagebüchern und Briefen*, 3 vols. (Leipzig 1902–8); trans. G. E. Hadow as *Clara Schumann, An Artist's Life* (London 1913).

Litzmann, Berthold, ed., *Clara Schumann–Johannes Brahms. Briefe aus den Jahren 1853–1896*, 2 vols. (Leipzig 1927; repr. Hildesheim and New York 1989).

May, Florence, *The Life of Brahms*, 2nd revised edn (London 1948).

McCorkle, Margit L., *Johannes Brahms. Thematisch-bibliographisches Werkverzeichnis* (Munich 1984).

Macfarren, George Alexander, Notes to the Programme of the Philharmonic Concert of London of 2 April, 1873.

Mies, Paul, 'Aus Brahms' Werkstatt', *Simrock Jahrbuch I* (Berlin 1928).

Müller Reuter, Theodor, *Lexicon der deutschen Konzertliteratur* (Leipzig 1921).

Musgrave, Michael, 'Historical Influences on Brahms's "Requiem"', *Music and Letters*, 53/1 (January 1972), pp. 3–17.

Musgrave, Michael, ed., *Brahms 2: Biographical, Documentary and Analytical Studies* (Cambridge 1985).

Neumark, Georg, *Fortgepflantzter Musikalisch-Poetischer Lustwald* (Jena, 1657).

Newman, William S., 'A "Basic Motive" in Brahms's "German Requiem"', *Music Review*, 24 (1963), p. 190.

Niemann, Walter, *Johannes Brahms* (Berlin 1920); trans. C. A. Phillips as *Brahms* (New York 1929).

Norrington, Roger, 'Old Habits die Hard', *Gramophone* (April 1990), pp. 1765–7.
'Aimez-vous Brahms?', *Gramophone* (October 1991), pp. 67–8.

Ochs, Siegfried, preface to Brahms, *A German Requiem*, op. 45, Eulenburg Edition No. 969, p. iv.
Geschehenes, Gesehenes (Leipzig 1922).
Das deutsche Gesangverein für gemischten Chor, 3 vols. (Berlin 1923–6).

Pascall, Robert, 'Historical Perspectives on Brahms's Ein deutsches Requiem', notes to the Norrington recording of Brahms's *German Requiem* EMI CD CDC754658–2, pp. 2–8.
'The Organ and Contrafagotto in Brahms's German Requiem'; letter to the editor, *The Musical Times*, 133 (January 1992), p. 7.

Reynolds, Christopher, 'A Choral Symphony by Brahms?', *Nineteenth-Century Music*, 9/1 (1985), pp. 3–25.

Russell, A. Tilden, 'Brahms and *Wer nur den lieben Gott läßt walten:* A New Contribution', *Newsletter of the American Brahms Society*, 6/2 (Autumn 1988).

Schubring, Adolf, '"Schumanniana Nr. 12": Ein deutsches Requiem . . . von Johannes Brahms', *Allgemeine musikalische Zeitung*, 4/2–3 (January 1869), pp. 9–11, 19–20.

Shaw, G. B., *Shaw's Music*, ed. Dan H. Laurence, 3 vols. (London 1981).

Specht, Richard, *Johannes Brahms. Leben und Werk eines deutschen Meisters* (Hellerau 1928), trans. E. Blom as *Johannes Brahms* (London 1930).

Steiner, A., *Johannes Brahms, 1. Teil. 86. Neujahrsblatt der Allgemeine Musikgesellschaft in Zürich* (Zurich 1898), p. 21.

Struck, Michael, 'Ein deutsches Requiem – handlich gemacht. Der Klavierauszug und seine Stichvorlage', *Patrimonia*, 80 (1994), pp. 5—18.

Thibaut, A. F., *Über Reinheit der Tonkunst* (Heidelberg 1825); trans. J. Broadhouse as *Purity in Music* (London 1882).

Tovey, Donald Francis, *Essays in Musical Analysis*, 6 vols. (London 1935–9); vol. V, *Vocal Music*.

Wagner, Richard, *The Prose Works of Richard Wagner*, trans. W. A. Ellis, 8 vols. (London 1892–9), vol. VI, *Religion and Art*.

Winterfeld, Carl von, *Johannes Gabrieli und sein Zeitalter* (Berlin 1843).

Zeileis, Friedrich G., 'Two Manuscript Sources of Brahms's German Requiem', *Music and Letters*, 60 (1979), pp. 149–55.

Index